THE TIMES
GUIDE TO
BUYING A
HOUSE

By CHARLES SHEA

PUBLISHED BY
TIMES NEWSPAPERS LIMITED

© Charles Shea 1970, 1971
Revised edition July 1971
Cover design by Jeanette Collins.
Cover illustration by Alan Cracknell.
Printed by C. Nicholls & Company Ltd.,
The Philips Park Press, Manchester.
7230 0010 7

CONTENTS

INTRODUCTION

THIS BOOK DOES NOT cover house purchase in Scotland and Northern Ireland. However, it contains all the information anyone needs for buying a house, flat or maisonette in England or Wales.

Housebuying is a complicated business but this book has been planned and written in such a way that the reader will find it easy to understand. If you begin at *Chapter 1* and read through to the end of *Chapter 8* you will have learnt all you need to know to find a mortgage and buy a home.

There are two places where you might find the going a bit hard. One is *tax relief* in *Chapter 5* and the other is *special mortgage schemes* in *Chapter 6*. You can miss these out on a first reading or skip them altogether if you are only interested in an ordinary mortgage arrangement.

The book has twelve chapters altogether. After the first eight come chapters on modernising an old house, having a house built, and getting a house through a housing group. The twelfth chapter is a glossary of terms like 'covenant' and 'road charges' and 'title' and 'planning permission' which have occurred in the text.

There are pictures, charts and diagrams throughout the book, and another thing you will find helpful is that where a term like 'valuation' or 'leasehold' occurs you will see a cross-reference guiding you to the page or chapter elsewhere in the book where the subject is discussed in detail.

If you are a quite well off person you may be intrigued to discover that the book pays much attention to the situation of people seeking to buy a house with not much money in hand and not a very high income, and that it examines cases, for example, where a mortgage loan of only £3500 or so is involved. This is only practical: many first-time housebuyers are not very well placed financially. But, that noted, the book has been devised for everyone and its exposition of the housebuying process has been framed to guide and inform buyers at all price levels.

CHAPTER ONE

CHOOSING A HOUSE

YOU NEED HAVE LITTLE TROUBLE finding a house to buy. There are about seven million private homes in Britain. About two hundred and eighty thousand of them come up for sale every year. Additionally about two hundred thousand or so new houses are built for private sale between every January 1 and December 31.

That's a lot of houses. One of them is going to be yours. Which one?

Obviously you can't look at them all. Perhaps the perfectionist viewing record is that claimed by Mr Reginald Slade, a businessman, who as a young married man looked at fifty-one houses before he found the one he liked. You are unlikely to want to be so thorough; a normal number of viewings would be from six to ten. We list *Ten ways of finding houses* on *page 18*.

The probability is that you will find a house to suit you within three months of beginning your quest. It may take longer, possibly six months or more, but unless you are under pressure it need not be other than interesting, certainly far from tedious.

However, you won't want to waste time and money travelling here and there to look at houses without a plan, and you will not do so if you make out a sensible scheme of operations and follow it.

First, decide where you want to live. This may be difficult because there can be any number of attractive reasons for wanting to live in a number of different places. The important thing is to get your thinking straight and put first things first.

The house must be convenient for your work

Your job is what will pay for the house—and the quality of the life you will have in it—and the priority is to ensure that you can leave every morning and return every evening from Monday to Friday week in and week out by a short, or quick, comfortable journey. Your chosen house must be so located that you can get to and from your work easily.

A good way of going about it is to get a map or draw one. In the middle of the map you put a mark representing where you work. Draw a large circle round it representing the area of the town. Within this circle mark areas where you know or guess that houses are for sale. You can leave out areas you don't like or know to be too expensive or rundown. Look at the others and jot down details of bus or train journey times, putting in fares too if you like.

Then draw a circle round the first one to represent the surrounding region and on it mark the spots, including other towns, where you might like to live and where there are likely to be houses you can afford to buy. Again mark in travelling times and fares.

Nearest is not always quickest

Don't assume that a spot on your map which lies closer to your work than others is easier and quicker to get to and from. In the case of such an area lying within your first circle—the one representing your town—it may prove that you would have to make one or two changes of bus or train in getting in and out. When you look at areas within your larger circle similarly remember that further-flung places served by fast trains or reached directly from a main station will be much quicker to get to and from than nearer places on a branch line.

Here is an example. Hounslow in Middlesex is 11 miles out of London. Reading in Berkshire is 36 miles out of London. You would think that anyone buying a house in Hounslow would enjoy a shorter journey into town. But that is not so. The tube train journey from Hounslow to Victoria at peak times is 40 to 45 minutes. The main line journey from Reading to Paddington is 28 to 30 minutes.

The map (*opposite*) is a clever illustration of the point that 'nearer is not necessarily quicker'. It is again an example based on travel to and from the capital. The map is drawn on a travelling-time scale the basis of which is the mile-a-minute London to Brighton rail journey. The light dots represent the actual location of towns: the black dots represent where they would be if placed in relation to journey time instead of distance. You will see that Dorking, which lies rather further from London than Banstead, is actually slightly quicker to reach. Sevenoaks, not much further away from London than Farningham, takes much longer to reach.

If you run a car you will attach more importance to roads and highway routes than to bus and train services: but your car will have to be serviced now and again and then you will be dependent on public transport for a while, so you cannot leave it out of reckoning altogether.

In considering the question of travelling time to work, you will naturally take into account the cost of fares or petrol. But

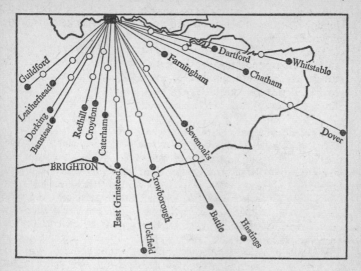

curiously this expenditure is not likely to be noted by a building society* in its scrutiny of your outgoings on a house you propose to buy. So it may happen that you will be attracted to buying a house some way out of a town or city because it is cheaper and because the cost of fares will not be reckoned against you in the mortgage calculations. Thus, for a somewhat desperate reason, you may discount the importance of being able to travel quickly and comfortably to your work every day. But it remains important all the same.

The district must suit your wife
Next come the things important to a woman, which may be rated as equal to a man's need of convenient travel to work. There are a number of them.

Your chosen house should be located so that she can make a convenient bus or train journey to her family and friends. It should stand near or among other houses where families like her own are living.

It should have near it a chemist's, a grocery, a butcher's, a

---

* In this book we will use the term 'building society' in connection with mortgages as a matter of convenience, but of course mortgages can be got from a number of other sources apart from building societies as you will see explained in detail in Chapter 4.

greengrocer's. It should not be more than a bus journey away, or a 20-minute or 25-minute drive, from supermarkets and larger stores in a general shopping centre.

It should be near a doctor and a dentist's.

If you have children, or are starting a family, it should be near a clinic and not far from a general hospital. It should be near a nursery and so located that children can reach school easily and without having to cross busy roads.

Schools policy is an important consideration

If you have children at or near secondary school age you should bear in mind that your chosen house should be in a district where they can go to the sort of school you would like them to attend. Educational policy varies from district to district: in some areas comprehensive schools are established, in others differing forms of schooling exist. This is something to take into account. To find out the educational policy in a district where you are thinking of choosing a house ask the local council, the county council, or write to or telephone the editor of the local paper.

The district must offer you things to do

Ask yourself what the district offers to interest and amuse you and your family in your leisure hours. A number of things enrich people's lives outside their work—golf, cricket, soccer, tennis, badminton, bridge, chess, dancing, going to the cinema, seeing plays, amateur dramatics, club photography, dining out, community activity, social work, singing in the choir, athletics, boxing, going to church, music, painting, concert going. Your chosen house should be placed to allow you to do what you like doing: if it is not you will feel the deprivation after a while.

Your house should be near to open space or parkland. If you are great readers the fact of a library being near may count very much with you.

The district must be a good one

The first three rules for choosing a house, you will have noted, lay emphasis on convenience and quality of living. Your house will be a disappointment to you no matter how nice it is if you have to spend three hours a day getting in and out to work; if your wife never sees a dress shop; if the neighbours are elderly while you are young; if your children pine for a playground; and if you never do anything, individually or together, because there is nothing on hand for you to do.

But obviously this isn't the all of it. The character of the district is important. If the neighbourhood is a poor one your house will be a poor buy.

You can investigate the neighbourhood on foot or on a bicycle, or in a car if you travel slowly and look about you carefully. Ask yourself these questions:

Is the district improving or deteriorating? The signs that a district is going down in the world are shabby houses, neglected gardens, broken fencing, litter on open spaces, empty houses, houses divided into flats, houses used as offices, gardens, yards or areas used for casual storage or commercial storage, spaces or frontages used for car mending.

Is the neighbourhood strictly residential? If it is not you will see workshops, offices, a laundry depot perhaps, a lorry park, cafes, a tyre dump, a businessmen's club, a garage.

Is the location peaceful? Highways, trunk roads, motorways near the house will suggest to you that it is not. A railway may run near by. An airport within a few miles will mean noise. A football ground or a stadium near by will mean crowds and traffic. A busy pub or a dance hall may mean disturbance at night and at weekends. A school very close will mean playground noise in mid-morning, at lunchtime and in mid-afternoon. A small park or council playground close to the house will mean noise in evenings and at weekends.

Is the district clean? If factories or railway yards or a brickworks lie in the wrong quarter in relation to the house, smut carried by the prevailing wind will make it dirty.

If your reconnaissance makes it clear that some or many of these unpleasant features exist the sensible thing to do is go and look for another house in another of your likely areas as marked on your map. You may find this hard to do if you have set your heart on a house, telling yourself that nuisance, unattractiveness or noise need not prove unduly obtrusive. But if you notice disagreeable things at this stage when you are under the first spell of the house you will notice them more keenly when you have settled in and the charm has begun to wear off. You must tell yourself that even if you think you can put up with the disadvantages, future buyers may well decide that they could not and the house will prove hard to sell later on, or you may have to sell at a loss.

However, let us assume that your investigation has shown the neighbourhood to be a good one. You now pay particular attention to the immediate surroundings of the house.

The house must be well sited

If the house is reached by a neat and pleasant road this is in its favour. If it has open space or good views about it this too is in its favour; but later on you or your solicitor must check (see *Chapter 2*) that there are no plans for buildings to go up which may block the view or alter the pleasant character of the surroundings. If the road has verges and is lined with trees this will add to the pleasure of living in it. If it is wide rather than narrow, and curving rather than straight, these are agreeable things also. If electricity wires, rediffusion wires or telephone wires are prominent between poles and to the front of houses this is a disagreeable feature.

Look at the neighbouring houses and, without being obtrusive about it, look at the neighbours.

If the house is on a hill the aspect may be the more open, free and pleasant, but you will be more exposed on windy and wintry days. You may not relish the thought of trudging up a hill after a day's work or an evening out, nor your wife after shopping, taking the children to school or taking the baby out in the pram.

If the area is hilly and the house stands on the northerly side of high ground it will be comparatively sunless and not very cheerful. If the house stands in the lower parts of hilly ground, fog and mist will come down from time to time: the subsoil may drain poorly, making the house damp: and there may be a risk of flooding. Avoid frost pockets.

It is best if the house stands on a level site. A steep gradient up to the house may offer difficulties with parking a car; a steep slope down to the house may produce drainage problems. Steep drives and paths are hazardous when ice forms in cold spells. Turning a car into and out of a sloping drive is difficult.

The house should have a carport or parking space or garage, or space for building a garage; and a garage should be wide enough to take your car and allow room for the opening of driver's door and passenger's door.

The garden should be large enough for your recreation and for storage of tools and bicycles, but not so large that it will be a burden to keep up. It should be properly fenced and have paths laid to all the access doors. The paths should be level, even and uncracked. If they are split, cracked or fallen in, the subsoil may be unstable—meaning that it shifts in different weather conditions or that the site is made-up ground, that is ground reclaimed from old mineral workings, former rubbish tips or swamp.

The house must be the right size and comfortable
When you view the house ask yourself these questions:

Is it light or dark? It is best if the living rooms face south-east to west. Bedrooms best face east to south. A kitchen is most pleasant when it faces east to south. The bathroom may face north-east to east, as it does not need sun.

Are the rooms big enough for your furniture and for comfortable family use?

Is there a lobby? Is the hall big enough to take a pram? Is there hanging space for coats?

Is there a utility room or storage area on the ground floor? Is there a workroom or space for a workbench?

Is the kitchen big enough for the family to have meals in there? Is the working area clear of people going in and out? Is the kitchen well ventilated?

Is there provision for drying clothes inside the house? Is there a warmed linen cupboard?

Is there a fuel store and is it under cover? Where does the dustbin stand?

Is there a second lavatory on ground floor level?

Can all windows be opened easily? Can they be cleaned easily? Are the upper windows safe for children?

Are window fastenings in good condition? Are all locks secure?

Is there a hot water system? Is it insulated at the cylinder and along lengths of pipes?

Is the water storage adequate? A 60-gallon cold tank is recommended for normal family use.

Is the house noisy or quiet? Can you hear the neighbours through the wall? Is the plumbing noisy?

Is there central heating? How much does it cost to run according to the owner's recent bills?

Is the roof space insulated to prevent loss of heat through ceilings? Is the piping system lagged against freezing at susceptible places? Are windows draught-proofed or double-glazed? Are draughts noticeable in the living rooms?

Can the loft be used for storage? Is there a light up there?

Are there enough electric points? There should be at least three in the living room, one in a dining room, four in a kitchen, two in a laundry or utility room, two in each bedroom, one at each level of hall and landing, one in a garage, one in a workshop.

What are the monthly rates?*

The price must be right
You have satisfied yourself that you have found the right house in the right district. Now you must ask yourself 'Is the price right?'

When the seller of a house tells you his price you should not say or imply that you necessarily accept it. Most people put a higher price up when they are selling than they actually expect to get and you will probably be able to negotiate a reduction. Bearing that in mind compare the seller's price with that of similar houses in the same street if you can or in a similar locality. If you are buying in midsummer or at the end of the year when the buying market is relatively slack you are more likely to get the price reduced. If you can promise speedy completion of the deal you will also be better placed to knock down the price. Also if a low valuation is placed on the house

---

* *See Glossary.*

(see later) or a surveyor's inspection reveals faults in it (*see Chapter 3*) you can make that the basis for asking for the price to be reduced.

Now you set about making the house yours.

You make an offer 'subject to contract'

Now—or you may have done it at any earlier point—you will make an offer to buy 'subject to contract'. Any token you may make in these early stages should be 'subject to contract', a simple phrase which ensures that you will not be committed to go ahead with the purchase of the house until you are satisfied on all counts that you can do so wisely, at which point you will enter into a binding contract to buy. It is best to have had a general discussion with a solicitor before even having begun to look for a house (see later) but whether or not you have done so the procedure at this stage will be the same.

You hand over a 'deposit to a stakeholder'

You accompany your 'subject to contract' offer with a cheque or cash as 'deposit to stakeholder' which helps establish you in the seller's eyes as a serious party and encourages him to keep the house 'under offer' to you. The deposit is best kept to a nominal level, say £30 or £50, and you should hand it not to the seller but to another person—an estate agent or solicitor, say—on the understanding that his role is that of a stakeholder, not agent for the seller. This is important. A stakeholder is a neutral party, holding the deposit in trust between you and the seller, and he may not pass it on to the seller without your written permission in the form of a deposit release. In contrast someone who receives the deposit as agent for the seller may yield it to the seller any time he asks for it: and so it can happen that the money gets into the seller's hands prematurely and stays there even if the deal falls through, and you have trouble getting it back.

There is not much point in making the 'deposit to stakeholder' as much as 10 per cent of the seller's asking price, as is often suggested, if you can avoid it. The sum can be made up to 10 per cent when the time comes to exchange contracts (*Chapter 2*), the point at which you and the seller commit yourselves to go ahead with the deal. Of course, whatever the sum you pay as 'deposit to stakeholder' make sure you get a receipt.

There are two things to be especially careful of with regard to 'deposit to stakeholder':

If you do eventually decide to buy the house make sure

that the 'deposit to stakeholder' is not overlooked or forgotten—in other words, make sure that it is counted as being part of your cash contribution (the down payment or deposit) towards the full purchase price (*see Chapter 5, page 56*).

If the deal falls through make sure you get your 'deposit to stakeholder' returned to you. People are sometimes bluffed or frightened into believing they have forfeited their 'deposit to stakeholder' or that it has been used up in expenses or something like that. An estate agent or other person professionally involved in the buying and selling of houses may be quite unscrupulous on the point, and so the warning is necessary.

It would be possible to write at length about sharp practice by estate agents dealing with inexperienced housebuyers, but it would hardly be fair to the great number who deal honestly and fairly day by day. Attempts to regularise and supervise the profession have so far proved unavailing and until the position is changed the only reasonable advice that can be given to the housebuyer over 'deposit to stakeholder' or anything else involving an agent is, deal with him alertly, keeping always in mind the possibility of him trying to be sharp at your expense. Letters behind an agent's name are some indication of professional reliability and schemes for safeguarding of deposits may be in operation by the initiative of the institution concerned. Letters are FRICS, FLAS, FAI, FSVA, FIAS, FRVA, FFAS or FFS, MNAEA.

You arrange for a valuation
Your next step is to ask a building society to make a valuation inspection of the house and tell you how much they will lend on it.

You may be hoping for a mortgage loan of 90 or 95 per cent of the price but you will be unusually favoured if you get it. The usual offer is about 80 per cent, and that will be 80 per cent of valuation not of price. A building society may give a valuation equal to price but more often valuation is below price, by a small or larger margin.

Valuation is high on modern houses of conventional design and good construction. It is lower on between-the-wars houses or houses not judged well built or favoured in their location: or of unusual or unconventional design. It is lower also on leasehold properties with much of the lease used up (*see Chapter 7*) and on flats and maisonettes (*see Chapter 8*), especially those produced by the conversion of an existing house, not custom-built. It will be lowest of all on pre-1919 houses with disadvantages—like short lease, poor neighbourhood, in a rundown state—in addition to their age.

An accompaniment of a low valuation may be a shortening of the mortgage repayment period, from 25 or 20 years to 20 or 15, and a higher interest rate* may be charged than the usual 8½ per cent.

If the building society gives a low valuation on your chosen house then this means that it does not think much of the house, or the area, and that it is not very confident of the chances of selling it later on at a good price. Tell the seller that the valuation is low and ask him if he will bring his price down. If he won't, probably the best thing is to call the whole thing off and look at another house. You may have no choice but to do this anyway. The lower the valuation the more you will have to find in cash to make up the buying figure, and you may find that the gap is too big for you to meet.

You will have to pay the building society a fee for sending an inspector to make the valuation, and the society will ask you to pay the fee in advance (*see also Chapter 2*). You may get half the fee back if the building society declines to offer any kind of loan on the house at all: but if it makes an offer and you decline it or it makes an offer which is too low to be of use to you you will get none of it back. The valuation fee on a £5000 house is about £10.

Remember that a valuation is not intended to give you any kind of guarantee that the house is sound and in good order. It is merely the building society's way of estimating what the house would fetch if the mortgage arrangement broke down and the house had to be sold quickly for the society to get its money back.

You have the house surveyed

You ask a professional surveyor to visit the house and give you a report on its condition (*see Chapter 3*). As with a low valuation if the surveyor finds things wrong which are going to cost money to put right you may ask the seller to drop his price to take account of this. This inspection, of course, is the one you *can* rely on to put your mind at rest about the condition of the

---

* *See Glossary.*

house. You can think of it as the equivalent to calling in the AA to make a thorough inspection of a secondhand car before you commit yourself to buy it. If the surveyor makes a mistake somewhere and you are subsequently put to unforeseen expense you make be able to claim damages from him. That is the measure of the high value of having a survey done.

The fee for a survey may be between £25 and £45 for an ordinary house, and there may be extra charges for a drains test and electrics test (*see Chapter 3, page 33*). You can get the names of surveyors in your district by writing to the Royal Institution of Chartered Surveyors, 12 Great George Street, London SW1; or the Incorporated Society of Valuers and Auctioneers, 3 Cadogan Gate, London SW1; or the Incorporated Association of Architects and Surveyors, 29 Belgrave Square, London SW1. An architect can undertake a survey for you: write to the Royal Institute of British Architects, 66 Portland Place, London W1.

You may find a surveyor through a local estate agent. But never let the seller's estate agent arrange a survey for you, because his job is to look after the seller's interests not yours. Obviously it is sensible to ask the surveyor what his fee is going to be before you engage him.

If you happen to be using the National Houseowners Society (*see Chapter 2, page 30*) to arrange the transfer of ownership of the house and the house is in or near London you can ask them to arrange a survey for you. The charge is very low, £6, plus the surveyor's travelling expenses. I had my house in London surveyed through this organisation and I have to say that a very thorough job was done. That need not be taken as a recommendation, simply an observation based on one successful experience.

You engage a solicitor

Unless you have it in mind to do the legal work involved in buying the house yourself, it is best to meet a solicitor for a discussion even before you start looking for a house. Thereafter you can keep him informed of your progress and when you have settled on a house you like you can ask him to start on the legal work: and he will have the advantage of knowing something about you already.

Ask the solicitor early on roughly what his charges are likely to be for his legal work on a house in the price range you are thinking of; and as soon as you know the purchase price and other details of your chosen house, and the details of the mort-

You can buy this pleasant house for £3150 in Mansfield, Notts. But at Bagshot, Surrey, you would pay £6000 for it. The difference in price is mainly due to the difference in the availability and cost of land in the two places, and demand for houses has something to do with it as well. Such differences in price between new houses—the one illustrated is a popular three-bedroom type—applies also to secondhand houses. The contrast between the Mansfield price and the Bagshot price for this particular house is the most dramatic, but to fill in the picture here are prices Wimpeys put on it in some other places: Northallerton, Yorks. £3450, Dumfries £3775, Preston £3850, Plymouth £4275, Studley, Warwickshire, £4450, Dunstable £5495.

From a photograph by George Wimpey & Co.

gage, give him all this information and ask him to tell you what his charges will be precisely. Don't imagine that this will offend him. You can take it that he will be pleased to have your business and he will approve of your practical approach, as it shows him that you are a decisive person who does not haver and hover and will not be a bother to him while he is busy working on your behalf once the buying process is under way.

You may know of a solicitor, or you may be recommended to one by your parents, relatives, friends, employer, bank manager, or an estate agent you meet while looking for a house. You can ask for the names and addresses of local solicitors at the Citizens Advice Bureau, or consult the Law List at your local library, or write to the Law Society, 113 Chancery Lane, London WC2.

We mentioned earlier, in connection with the survey, the

National Houseowners Society. This is an organisation which undertakes the equivalent of a solicitor's work in house transactions but at a lower fee. It is referred to in the next chapter, *Chapter 2*, in which we will be examining the costs involved in the purchase of a house.

Ten ways of finding houses

Through estate agents. Write or call as many estate agents as you can asking them what houses they have on their books in your preferred districts at the price you want to pay. This service is free to you because the estate agents look to sellers of houses to pay them for getting houses sold. On the other hand, the service is not entirely reliable for you. An estate agent, or anybody selling a house, is restrained from actually saying untrue things about the house but without breaking the law he can describe it in terms which are overenthusiastic or omit to mention disadvantages: in short, he may give a one-sided picture. If you like the general description of a house but think the information given by the agent in his circular is incomplete (or you suspect that it is unbalanced) telephone him and ask for more information before setting out to have a look at the place, and you may save yourself a pointless journey. If you can telephone the owner direct, so much the better.

You can find a house through newspaper advertisements— local papers, regional papers, national Sunday papers like the *Sunday Times*, the *Observer*, the *Sunday Telegraph*, daily papers like *The Times*, the *Daily Telegraph*. You can look in *The Lady*, *Exchange and Mart*, *Dalton's Weekly*, the *London Weekly Advertiser*. In London, the *Evening News* and *Evening Standard* carry regular house advertisement sections. The *Daily Mail* has a house advertisement section with illustrations of houses offered. There are a number of magazines published specifically for houseseekers: *Homefinder, New Homes and Conversions, Housebuyer, Homehunters Weekly*.

You can find a house by going round your preferred districts looking for For Sale boards. If you see an empty house which you like the look of but has no board you can trace the owner by asking the neighbours, the postman or milkman, or by inquiring at the rating department at the local council offices.

You can find a house by asking your local council if it has properties to sell, or if it runs a property register of houses for sale. In London you can ask the Greater London Council, County Hall, London, SE1, if it has houses for sale, and of course you can do the same of the authorities in other big cities. The GLC, and perhaps other large authorities, at any one time may have houses to dispose of where previous buyers using the council's mortgages scheme have been dispossessed.

You can find a new home through the Housing Enquiry Service of Duke Street House, 415–417 Oxford Street, London W1R 2BD. This service, which lists new houses on estates in all parts of the country, is run by a firm of insurance brokers, Barnet Gold & Co., but using it does not put you under any obligation to them.

You can find a new house by visiting the New Homes Show organised in London every year by Homefinder (1915) Ltd, of 199 Strand, London WC2; or in the Midlands by visiting the Midlands New Home shows organised by Midland Homehunter, Kingsford House, 202 Wolverhampton Street, Dudley, Worcs.

You can find a house by looking at notices of auction. If you make an offer before the auction date you may be able to buy privately and avoid having to compete with other bidders in a sale room. If the house you want does come up at auction it may be withdrawn because the bidding fails to reach the reserve price, that is the lowest price the seller will accept, and in that case you can ask the auctioneer afterwards what the reserve price is and make an offer at that level if you judge it worthwhile. *But do not actually bid at an auction* unless you are quite sure what you are about. Your bid, if successful, is binding on you: you cannot wriggle out of it: and if you have not gone about the matter properly you may find yourself in a mess. Never set out with the idea of getting a house through an auction without having a consultation with a solicitor well in advance of the auction date.

You can find a house to buy in the designated area of a New Town by writing to the development corporations of the town or to the Commission for New Towns. You may only be eligible if you intend to work in the town, but sometimes this rule is waived and additionally a development corporation may be able to give you a mortgage. For the New Towns of Crawley, Hemel Hempstead and Hatfield and Welwyn write to the Commission for New Towns, Glen House, Stag Place, London SW1. For the following New Towns write to the development corporation in the town near to you or which specially interests you: *England* Aycliffe, Co. Durham; Basildon, Essex; Bracknell, Herts; Corby, Northants; Harlow, Essex; Milton Keynes, Bucks; Northampton; Peterborough, Hunts; Peterlee, Co. Durham; Redditch, Worcs; Runcorn, Cheshire; Skelmersdale, Lancs; Stevenage, Herts; Telford, Shropshire; Warrington, Lancs. *Wales* Cwmbran, Mon; Newtown, Montgomeryshire. *Scotland* Cumbernauld, Dumbartonshire; East Kilbride, Lanarkshire; Glenrothes, Fife; Irvine, Ayshire; Livingston, Midlothian.

You can find a house by advertising in a newspaper covering the areas where you want to live. Here is how to word it: 'Modern house wanted, Bestside area, by private buyer. Three bedrooms, garage, good garden. About £4200'. Give your name and address and telephone number because if you use a box number people will suspect that you are an estate agent using this form of canvassing to get more properties on his books and you will have fewer replies.

CHAPTER TWO

THE COSTS OF BUYING A HOUSE

IN THE DAYS WHEN HOUSEOWNING WAS for the few, people paid the cash costs associated with house purchase apparently without a thought. Now, with nearly half of all Britain's families owning their homes and the proportion increasing, you often hear criticism expressed of all the charges, fees, expenses and tolls that a housebuyer has to pay.

What are these costs? Are there ways in which they can be avoided or reduced?

We have mentioned two of them already—valuation fees, survey fees. Let's look at the whole picture now: let us see what the housebuyer gets for his money and whether it is money well spent.

At the same time let us trace the process by which a housebuyer makes the house his. We have already discussed this to some extent in *Chapter 1*, but now we will complete the picture, with special reference to a solicitor's work and to surveying, and put the whole thing in the context of costs.

To make it more practical, let's put ourselves in the place of a family buying a house for the first time and see how their costs fall out. This family—let's give them a name: the Hunters—have seen a house they want at the price they have in mind, £4250.

The first unavoidable expense is the valuation fee

The Hunters ask the building society for a mortgage on the house and the society sends an inspector to make a valuation. The valuation fee for a house of this price is about £10 and the Hunters are also asked to meet the inspector's travelling expenses at 9d a mile.

The expense is unavoidable. Whoever is approached for a mortgage for a house—building society or some other lender (*see Chapter 4*)—a valuation will be carried out and the buyer must pay the fee.

The next cash commitment is the difference between valuation and price . . .

The valuation proves to be £4100 and the Hunters at least now know how they stand on that score. They will have to make up the balance of £150 in cash.

... and the difference between mortgage offer and valuation

In notifying the Hunters of the valuation figure of £4100 the building society enclosed a 'letter of acceptance'* offering a mortgage of 80 per cent of this figure. This is somewhat lower than the Hunters had expected, but after phoning the building society manager Mr Hunter learns that the offer will be increased to 85 per cent under an insurance arrangement known as 'mortgage indemnity' (*see Chapter 5, page 59*). He decides to adopt this arrangement and accordingly the mortgage offer is increased to the 85 per cent level, meaning that Mr Hunter would have to contribute 15 per cent, £615, in cash, in addition to the £150 difference between valuation and price.

Next: Premium on mortgage indemnity policy

The mortgage indemnity arrangement involves an insurance policy, the cost of which falls on Mr Hunter. The building society arranges this policy for him and informs him that the cost is a single premium which is worked out by charging £4 10s for every £100 guaranteed under the indemnity arrangement (*see Chapter 5, page 59*). In Mr Hunter's case the sum guaranteed is £205, the difference between 80 per cent and 85 per cent of £4100, and so the charge to him is £9. The building society offers to include this small sum in the mortgage loan and Mr Hunter agrees, glad to get one item, even if it is only a small one, out of the way.

It may be possible to get the price reduced

He is more concerned about the sums of £615 and £150 he must pay towards the purchase price out of his own cash resources. He had not expected that the valuation would be only £4100; and the total cash deposit of £765 is about a hundred pounds more than he had thought he would have to find. Accordingly he asks the seller to reduce his price. He has strengthened his hand by having a survey made (*see Chapter 3*), which has revealed faults in the house, and he succeeds in getting a reduction of £100.

Survey fee is another expense

The survey Mr Hunter had had carried out on the house cost him £25 plus £5 for a drains test. His bill for survey fees could have been much higher than this because the family had been

---

* *See Glossary.*

General fees and costs

Purchase price of house £4250

SURVEY	VALUA-TION	DEPOSIT		
May include drains test and electrics test		Valuation figure proves to be £4100. Difference between this figure and price of house to be paid by buyer in cash	Building society offer loan as percentage of the valuation figure of £4100	
			85% offered leaving 15% of valuation figure to be paid by buyer in cash	**95%** offered leaving 5% of valuation figure to be paid by buyer in cash
£30	**£10**	**£150**	**£615**	**£205**

keen on two other houses and Mr Hunter had very nearly decided to have surveys made of those other two as well. However, after realising that this would add up to something like eighty or ninety pounds for three surveys, he decided to make a detailed preliminary inspection of each house for himself. What he found convinced him that two of the houses were inferior and so he dismissed them from his mind and commissioned a professional surveyor to make a really thorough and expert survey of the third and give him a full report.

It is impossible to maintain that money paid out for a professional survey is money ill-spent. It is not. But it is a pity to pay a succession of survey fees on a number of houses only one of which you are going to buy. Like Mr Hunter, you can avoid such duplication by doing some preliminary surveying on your own account. It is not an overwhelmingly difficult operation, as the guidance given in *Chapter 3* will show you.

The next items of expense the Hunters have to take account of are associated with the transfer of ownership of the house from the seller to them.

They had had a discussion with a solicitor early on and now that they had an offer of a mortgage and had settled the price with the seller they asked him to press on to get the purchase completed as quickly as possible.

Already the solicitor had been active in respect of the chosen house making local searches—the start of a long and complex investigation to ensure that all was as it should be with the property and that when Mr Hunter became the owner there would be no nasty surprises stored up for him, that he would indeed be the legal and proper owner, and so on. These searches and inquiries were to cover any development plans* for the neighbourhood which might affect the property, any compulsory purchase orders* or other official orders that might be in existence on the property, or local authority plans—like a new highway which might take a slice off the garden—any charges against the house. The solicitor was also to set himself to find out if there are any road charges* outstanding or due, whether there are covenants* or easements* which might affect the Hunters' use of the house and their enjoyment of it; and so on.

The solicitor has applied to the seller's solicitor for a draft contract*, has scrutinised it and has begun to ask the other solicitor questions arising from it. On the basis of this exchange of questions and answers a firm contract will be drawn up which Mr Hunter and the seller will sign.

This is all going to take some weeks, but eventually when Mr Hunter's solicitor is satisfied that all is as it should be up to this point, identical copies of the contract will be signed and exchanged between Mr Hunter and the seller, a 10 per cent deposit of £415 will be handed over by Mr Hunter, and the seller will be committed to sell and Mr Hunter will be committed to buy.

Another item of expense is a premium for fire insurance

When this stage, exchange of contracts, has been reached the responsibility for insuring the house will pass to Mr Hunter. He might try to avoid this small expense but it would be more than stupid of him because if the house suffered damage or were destroyed after exchange of contracts he would be left with a shell or a pile of scorched rubble and would still be obliged

---

* *See Glossary.*

to proceed with the purchase. Accordingly he will arrange insurance at the usual rate of 2s 6d for every £100 value of the house—a total premium of between £5 and £6.

After exchange of contracts the solicitor will enter the second stage of his work for Mr Hunter. He will investigate title*, making sure that the seller has a proper claim to the property, and carry out his final searches. He will prepare the draft deed of conveyance* and eventually engross (that is, make a fair copy of) the final version. He will examine the title deeds* and finally on Mr Hunter's behalf he will meet the other solicitor for completion* when, in brief, he will hand over the balance of the purchase price, collect the title deeds and take over the keys. Finally he will complete and stamp the documents and dispose of the last few formalities.

There may be small sums to pay the seller

As the date for completion draws near Mr and Mrs Hunter will be surprised at themselves to find what sharp attention they will be giving to quite small sums shown on the completion statement as being due to be paid by them to the seller.

These small sums, as their solicitor was to explain to them, were the apportionments—reimbursement to the seller for payments he had made beyond the completion date, which of course is the day on which the Hunters are to get the keys and take possession. Such payments would be on the score of rates* and water rates paid in advance. If the house were lease-hold (see Chapter 7) they might also include the items of ground rent and fire insurance premium paid in advance.

The Hunters as said were surprised at themselves and slightly amused at the way they scrutinised and checked these small sums on the completion statement. Here they were buying a house for thousands of pounds, putting hundreds of their own money in as deposit, nerving themselves to face the solicitor's bill for his work—yet checking quite insignificant amounts of pounds, shillings and pence. Such is human nature. Anyway, the solicitors had got it worked out to the last penny and it was all quite obviously in order at £8 6s 3d.

It is worth mentioning that items like gas, electricity and telephone charges did not figure in the apportionments. It had been agreed that the more sensible thing was to arrange for the meters to be read and the telephone account made up on

---

* See Glossary.

completion day; for the bills to be sent to the seller; and for the Hunters to commence using the services as new occupiers.

One other item that did figure on the completion statement was £40 to be paid to the seller for things he had agreed to leave in the house. These were a carpet, a free-standing dresser in the kitchen, and a rather splendid ceiling light fitting in the sitting room which Mrs Hunter had admired on sight. To make the arrangement regular, the Hunters told their solicitor of this agreement with the seller; and he noted it as something to be formally included in the contract.

Legal expenses must be met. Solicitor's fee—1
The house the Hunters are buying is a registered* property and freehold (*see Chapter 7*). On this basis the solicitor's fee for conveyancing* proves to be £41.

Solicitor's fee—2
The solicitor has also worked on the mortgage. His fee for this is £24.

Solicitor's minor fees and expenses
The solicitor also adds a sum to his bill to cover search fees and his out of pocket expenses. This comes to about £5.

Building society's solicitor's fee
All the time Mr Hunter's solicitor has been active another solicitor has been at work—the building society's solicitor— investigating and checking to ensure that the building society's interests are looked after. Mr Hunter has to pay his bill too— another £24.

However, Mr Hunter has slipped up here. Had he known it he could have asked the building society to suggest to him the name of a solicitor on the building society's 'approved' list. Such a solicitor could have worked on the mortgage jointly for Mr Hunter and the building society, and his fee would have been only £24. Well, Mr Hunter has lost the chance of saving £24 and there is nothing he can do about it now.

Stamp duty* must be paid
The house the Hunters are buying is less than £5500 in price and so there is no stamp duty to pay on the transfer of ownership.

---

* *See Glossary.*

Legal Fees

Purchase price of house £4250

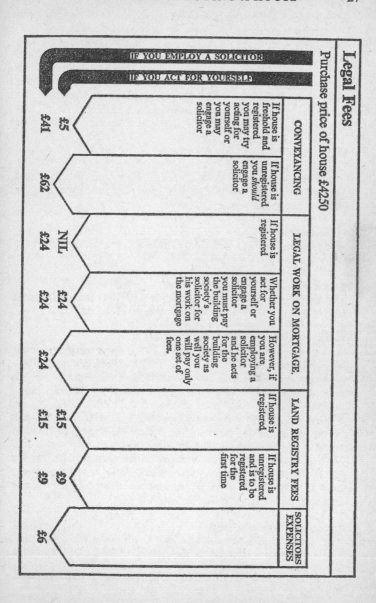

IF YOU EMPLOY A SOLICITOR

IF YOU ACT FOR YOURSELF

	CONVEYANCING		LEGAL WORK ON MORTGAGE.		LAND REGISTRY FEES		SOLICITORS EXPENSES
Description	If house is freehold and registered you may try acting for yourself or you may engage a solicitor	If house is unregistered you *should* engage a solicitor	If house is registered	Whether you act for yourself or employing a solicitor and he acts you must pay the building society's solicitor for his work on the mortgage — However, if you are employing a solicitor and he acts as well your building society will pay only one set of fees.		If house is registered	If house is unregistered and is to be registered for the first time	
IF YOU ACT FOR YOURSELF	£5		NIL	£24		£15	£9	
IF YOU EMPLOY A SOLICITOR	£41	£62	£24	£24		£15	£9	£6

Stamp duty used to be charged on the mortgage deed, by the way. The charge, though small, was realised to be a pointless encumbrance and it was abolished.

There is a Land Registry fee to pay as the house is registered*
The Hunters must also pay a fee for the transfer of ownership and the mortage to be registered at the Land Registry*— another £15. Again this is not solicitor's remuneration but a public service charge.

One more expense—premium on mortgage protection policy
Finally Mr Hunter has to arrange insurance cover which would clear the debt to the building society and leave his family debt-free if he dies before the mortgage is paid off. The building society advises him that a mortgage protection policy can be arranged for a single premium of a little over £100 (see Chapter 6, page 79). As happened over the mortgage indemnity policy premium, the building society manager says he is prepared to add this sum to the mortgage loan, and Mr Hunter gratefully agrees – although the thought does come into his mind that if the building society is ready to lend him another hundred pounds or so on this score it might have been a bit more generous and given him a bigger mortgage in the first place.

What it all adds up to
But perhaps it's as broad as it's long, he says to himself thinking it over some time later when, all arrangements long since completed and the family comfortable in their new home, he has a chance to reflect on the ins and outs of his housebuying operation. If the building society had lent him much more his monthly repayments on the mortgage would have been higher and as it is he finds that he can only just meet them without having to trim the family budget on other counts.

However, he is not entirely happy about all the costs he had to incur in buying the house. Running over them in his mind, as new houseowners are wont to do, he added them up again.

His own cash contribution had been £665. He didn't begrudge that because after all that could be regarded as a direct investment in the property.

The valuation fee of £10 seemed reasonable enough on the face of it, although Mr Hunter couldn't help wondering how many

---

* See Glossary.

inspections a building society inspector can get into a working day at £10 or so a visit.

The mortgage indemnity policy premium of £9 he judged to be a cheap price to pay for avoiding having to put down a bigger deposit. He knew that the survey fees of £30 were money well spent.

The £6 premium for fire insurance had been a necessary expense, obviously.

The apportionments of about £8 had been nothing more than fair reimbursement to the seller.

The Land Registry fees of £15 had had to be paid, Mr Hunter knew. The money went to pay for the Land Registry service, and there had been no chance of economising on this item.

The premium on the mortgage protection insurance policy might seem high at something over £100, he thought, but then it was a once and once only payment covering the whole of the mortgage term. And, as with the mortgage indemnity policy premium, it had been covered by an extra loan from the building society relieving him of having to pay it in cash.

Summing up totals so far, Mr Hunter listed his costs in three main parts: Deposit of £665: immediate cash expenses £69: expenses covered by an extra mortgage loan about £110.

Then there had been the solicitors' fees and expenses—about £65 to his own solicitor and £24 to the building society solicitor. Mr Hunter had been pleased and impressed with the patience and skill of his solicitor in dealing with what had seemed to him an incomprehensible rigmarole. But he could kick himself, he reflected, for learning too late that he might have shared a solicitor with the building society and saved that useful sum of £24.

Adding the two solicitors' charges to his previous figures he reached the sums that by now were as familiar to him as the front door of his family's new home: Direct cash outgoings £823: deferred costs £110: grand total £933.

Mr Hunter now calculated his direct cash outgoings as a percentage of the purchase price of £4150. It was 20 per cent.*

---

* This figure is interesting and important. It is exactly the average percentage of price that buyers do contribute in cash. We make this point because in following the Hunters' story you may have been thinking a bit vexedly that it bears little relation to your case – you being intent on buying at £3500 or £7000 or some other figure much different from £4150. The fact is that whatever price you buy at you can expect to have to contribute in cash between 15 per cent and 25 per cent of price: the lower level applying to new houses, the higher level to secondhand houses.

Could he have kept his costs any lower? Well, one rejoinder is that they might have been higher still. Had the house been unregistered* his solicitor's charge for conveyancing* would have been £62. Admittedly in that case the £15 Land Registry* fee would not have been called for but if the house had had to be registered for the first time on this transaction there would have been for a fee of about £9.

That said, let us note that . . .

It is possible to save on legal costs

The house being registered* and freehold, two conditions which simplify the legal work, Mr Hunter might have cut a solicitor out altogether and acted for himself, in which case his expenses would have been about £5 for postage, telephone, stationery and fares. But he would not have been well advised to do so unless he was quite sure he had the time and the level-headedness to cope with the mass of detail.

He might have reduced his expenses in another way, by employing the National Houseowners Society to carry out the work his solicitor did. This organisation, founded in 1963, offers a cut-price service to housebuyers and seems to have given consistent satisfaction to some thousands of clients. You should note that its staff are not lawyers and that its operations are opposed by the Law Society. If that does not deter you the southern address is 3 Railway Approach, Harrow, Middlesex, and that of the northern office is 4 Croxton Close, Sale, Cheshire.

Is a solicitor really necessary?

A timely word here about the solicitor's role in the housebuying process. Having followed the story of the Hunters you may be thinking that the solicitor's job is a very straight forward one and that he seems to collect a sizeable fee for just sitting in his office and going through a routine he has mastered as part of his law studies. Don't be deceived by the Hunters' story, however. The Hunters are imagined people and their case is not typical in its lack of complications. Few, very few, housebuying deals go through as smoothly as this, and it is when complications crop up that solicitors—or their highly experienced managing clerks— come into their own as expert resolvers of awkward problems, legal or human.

Let's say that Mrs Hunter had assumed without asking that

---

* *See Glossary.*

the free-standing dresser in the kitchen would be left behind as part of the fittings of the house: she would have been in for a shock and a disappointment to find on moving-in day that the seller was taking it away, as her solicitor would have advised her he had a perfect right to do. Let's take another point. Assume that Mr Hunter had his cash resources tied up in shares and that he failed to realise that the shares would have to be sold in good time for the 10 per cent deposit to be made up at the time of exchange of contracts. Part of his solicitor's work would be to remind him on the point—or, if there were any difficulty for any reason over producing cash on time to advise him about obtaining a temporary loan or meeting the contingency in some other way. Another case. Let's say that the Hunters, eager to get to work furnishing and decorating their new home, urged the seller to let them move in after exchange of contracts but before completion date. Such a move would raise a number of delicate points about the care of the house, payment to the seller for yielding possession early, and here again the solicitor's value would become evident. Or let's imagine that between exchange of contracts and completion the seller misused the house or garden, or stripped the garden of its bushes and plants, or in some other way spoiled things for the Hunters: they would look to their solicitor again, and rightly, to sort things out to their satisfaction, and this he would do for them as part of his service.

A most useful thing the specialist will do in the housebuying process is to ensure that the right sums of money are available and are paid over at the right junctures. This is routine, but if you still need convincing that there is more to the job than meets the eye, here are a few cases from life that ungainsayably make the point. Mr Alan Hamilton was set on buying a house at Purdhoe on Tyne, Northumberland, as the marriage home for himself and his fiancée. It was a very nice house, but there was one thing wrong that Mr Hamilton didn't know about and which his solicitor discovered for him—the local council was planning a new road right through the site. Mr Hamilton was disappointed at having to give up the house but relieved and grateful that he had been headed off from a doomed dwelling. Here is another story, not of 'what might have been' but of what rather grimly *was*. A builder bought a house at auction in a Hampshire town to find that he had become owner of a dwelling which, again, the local council had marked down for acquisition to make way for a road widening scheme—the kind of disastrous experience it is well worth paying a solicitor to avert. Once more story, that of a mysterious two square feet of land in the middle of the drive to a house at Kingswinford, Staffordshire. Mr Stanley Heath, who was in process of buying the house, had to delay his wedding plans because the tiny area apparently belonged to a third party and the building society refused to grant a mortgage until the matter was sorted out. It developed that the two square feet of drive belonged to the local authority. Mr Heath's solicitor got to work to sort the legal complications out to the satisfaction of the building society; and Mr Heath was able to proceed with the wedding arrangements, blessing the astuteness of Staffordshire solicitors while privately wondering at the way that human destinies may become dependent on such awkward trifles.

Going back to the Hunters, we might say that had Mr Hunter decided to save on his costs by dispensing with the specialist he might have run into more trouble than the saving was worth, and in the end might have had to take the half-finished business to a solicitor to begin anew and complete satisfactorily. All the same, as previously noted, a buyer can act for himself if the house is freehold and registered: it is simply that no one would actually *recommend* it as a thing to do.

In contrast, it is strong good sense to try to save money another way—by making a thorough preliminary survey of the houses you have it in mind to buy. In the story of the Hunters we have seen how payment of a succession of fees was avoided, and this is a good moment to study how such a preliminary survey is carried out.

CHAPTER THREE

SURVEYS AND PRELIMINARY SURVEYS

WE HAVE SEEN THAT the point of having a house surveyed before you buy it is to ensure that it is sound and in reasonably good order structurally. The older the house the more faults there are likely to be, but this does not mean that modern houses are free from faults and need not be surveyed.

Many houses built in the nineteen thirties were put up hurriedly by indifferent workmen using poor materials. There are other kinds of hazards apart from age and bad building: a house built two years ago in Devon was found to be in danger of having its foundations washed away by an underground current!

However, if a new house has been built under the supervision of an architect or chartered surveyor or the National House-Builders Registration Council* it is reasonable to dispense with a survey.

You can expect to pay up to about £45 for a comprehensive survey by a qualified man. If a drains test is done the surveyor will probably nominate a builder to do it, whose charge will be about £5. An electrics test will cost from about £1.50 or £2.

As advised earlier in this book never agree to the seller's estate agent arranging a survey on your behalf. Find your own surveyor from another estate agent or by writing to the addresses given in *Chapter 1, page 16*. When you meet the surveyor or speak to him on the phone mention that you would like him to give you an idea of what specific repair work may be needed on the house, with an estimate of the cost. It is on the basis of such information that you may be able to negotiate with the seller for a reduction in price, bearing in mind that the surveyor's estimate may or may not be accurate and that you will only be able to be sure of costs after comparing two or more estimates from builders.

Repair costs can be startling. On *page 35* you will see a sketch of a house showing a number of things that may be found wrong in the structure as will be shown in detail in this chapter. How much would it cost to have these faults put right? The sketch was studied by an Ealing, west London, builder, and he gave the answer in two parts. First, there are a number of jobs

---

* *See Glossary.*

where he felt able to give a reasonably firm, or not wildly varying, indication of what he would charge if called in. These are (*see sketch*) putting right defective flashings at chimney angle £20 to £25: sash windows £25 to £35: dampproofing boundary wall £15 to £25: bulging ceiling £50 to £80: dampproof course £200 to £300: airbricks £5 to £15: rewiring £100: ventilating stack £5 to £10.

Second, there are the jobs where he could do no more than give lower and upper figures some of which differed tremendously from each other. Roof tile defects, for example, might cost no more than £5 to put right or might cost £100. Rebuilding of gable wall might cost £250 or upwards to £500. Putting right faults in lead water piping would cost between £5 and £50. Damp penetration around windows might bring a £50 bill or one ranging up to £250. Attending to a worn balcony covering where damp has got in would be a job costing between £5 and £50 depending on the severity of the fault. Defective hanging tiles might be a £5 job or up to £20. Replacing an old cistern would cost from £25 to £50. Dealing with a sag in roof is a £50 to £100 job. The sagging boundary wall might cost only £10 to put right or might cost £60. A tilted lintel is a £5–£30 job, rusted gutters £5 to £50, ceiling-with-wall cracks £5 to £30, tilted window frames with corresponding interior cracks £5 to £60, a sloping bedroom floor £10 to £100.

Of course estimates from a jobbing builder in a country village would very likely be somewhat lower than the general level of the foregoing, but the point to be taken is not that repair work tends to be more expensive in London than elsewhere, as is obvious, but that the cost of rectifying faults in a house can only be surely reckoned after a builder's examination. As said, we advise that you arrange examination and get estimates from more than one builder, for all that this may be time-consuming or troublesome: and if in addition you have a set of rough estimates in hand from your surveyor you will be reasonably well placed to reach a sound conclusion about the likely costs of necessary repairs.

The advantages of a preliminary survey

Doing a preliminary survey yourself has two advantages. First, the results of your inspection should indicate whether it is worth-while going any further. Second, you will be better able to understand a professional surveyor's report after having had a good look at a house yourself.

You can equip yourself with some oldish clothes, a torch, a

What to watch out for when looking at a house

Gable wall bulging out. May need—rebuilding.

Bulge in ceiling indicating leak from cistern or pipes—or loosening of plaster key between laths.

Internal lead water piping sagging through inadequate support: Pin hole leaks in piping caused by action of lime.

Window flush with wall. Suspect damp penetration and rot in frames. Careful check of rear windows necessary—more liable to be neglected.

Electric wiring in house old and defective.

Flashing defective at angle of bay roof and house. Damp getting in.

Interior: Wood worm in under side of staircase and frame of understairs cupboard.

Airbricks blocked: ventilation for subfloor cut off helping spread of rot in joists and floorboards.

No damp proof course: Effect—rising damp, damage to internal decorating, rot.

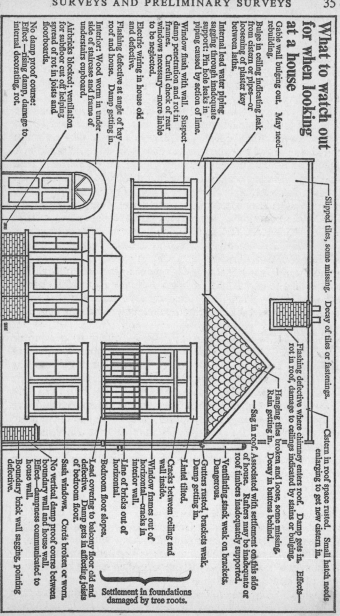

Slipped tiles, some missing. Decay of tiles or fastenings.

Flashing defective where chimney enters roof. Damp gets in, rot in roof, damage to ceilings indicated by stains or bulging.

Hanging tiles broken and loose, some missing. Rain getting in. Decay in battens behind.

Cistern in roof space rusted. Small hatch needs enlarging to get new cistern in. Effects—

Sag in roof. Associated with settlement on this side of house. Rafters may be inadequate or roof timbers inadequately supported.

Ventilating stack weak on brackets. Dangerous.

Gutters rusted, brackets weak. Damp getting in.

Lintel tilted.

Cracks between ceiling and wall inside.

Window frames out of horizontal—cracks in interior wall.

Line of bricks out of horizontal.

Bedroom floor slopes.

Lead covering to balcony floor old and defective. Damp gets in affecting joists of bedroom floor.

Sash windows. Cords broken or worn.

No vertical damp proof course between boundary wall and house wall. Effect—dampness communicated to house wall.

Boundary brick wall sagging, pointing defective.

Settlement in foundations damaged by tree roots.

screwdriver, binoculars for viewing roofs and high places from outside, marbles for detecting slopes in floors or a small spirit level. If there seems a touch of absurdity in these it no more than corresponds with the slight feeling of foolishness any ordinary person has in setting out to investigate the mysteries of someone else's house. If you think you would be too self-conscious to do the job properly don't do it at all. If you do do it however recognise yourself for what you are, an intelligent and determined amateur shaping up to a professional exercise, and proceed accordingly.

Take the weather into account

It is best to see a house empty and after a period of rain, but as regards the first point you will probably have to accept that the house is still occupied and furnished when you go to look at it. The house being empty does give you the best chance to go over it thoroughly but remember that if it has been standing empty for some while the characteristics of a fault like internal rising damp may have disappeared.

If an old house has been newly redecorated tell yourself to be suspicious. It is one thing for a seller to apply a lick of paint here and there to brighten up a house for selling, quite another for him to repaper a room to cover cracks which testify to the imminent disintegration of the place! Sometimes old houses are smartened up by a rendering being applied to the external walls— cement, pebbledash, stucco. It may seem unfair to be suspicious about this because such a job is not cheap, but the fact is that rendering is a very effective way of concealing cracks and so you should make a point of looking all the more intently for the internal clues that would confirm that the outer walls are in a bad way (see later).

Faith can sometimes triumph over suspicion

However, if it pays to be alert it may also pay to have simple faith that a well decorated house is just what it seems—as the story of the Ritchies shows. Two years married, Mr and Mrs Alan Ritchie were househunting in Essex, and in the little town of Billericay saw just the place they wanted. As they tell the tale today, the house was beautifully decorated and they were enchanted with it, but they began to have doubts after hearing what their surveyor had to say. He reported ground subsidence and warned them that almost certainly internal decorating had been carried out to conceal evidence of settlement and get the place sold. The seller protested that this was not so—the high standard of decoration in the house was simply the result of the attention he had given it as a good householder in the three years he had had it: he was only selling because the house had proved too big for him and his wife. The Ritchies hesitated, torn between their surveyor's certainty that there was something wrong and their great liking for the house and a feeling of trust they acknowledged for the seller. Their eventual decision was to take his word and go ahead with the deal, to the accompaniment of warnings of disaster from the surveyor. That was 16 years ago: no movement of any kind has occurred in the house structure: and the Ritchies, now the parents of five children, bless the day they backed their hunch about human nature and went ahead with the purchase of the house, a largish one, and its three acres of grounds. A pleasant story, proving that surveyors and their suspicions may sometimes be wrong even though thousands on thousands of times they are not.

Next—is the house damp?

Check, by asking or by taking measurements, that the house has cavity walls—that is, that the main walls are composed of two skins of bricks with a space, the cavity, between them. Check that the house has a dampproof course, which should be visible as a thin dark or grey line between courses of bricks about six inches above ground level. See that boundary walls or the walls of outside structures have dampproof courses, including a vertical one where a wall adjoins the house.

Look at the pointing—the mortar between the bricks—and if it is loose or crumbling note it as a fault and a possible cause of damp in the house. If the gutters at the eaves are rusted and weak suspect penetration of damp. Pay special attention to the south-west side of the house, which is most exposed to rain driven by wind. Examine the angles where balconies meet the house wall: where the top of bay windows meets the house: where the chimney enters the roof. These angles should be sealed with flashings or fillets, but the protective covering or substance may have deteriorated, letting damp in.

If the windows are not recessed into the wall but are flush with it, again suspect that damp has got in around the frames. Be particularly alert about windows at the back of the house, as usually they are not so well maintained as those at the front.

The roof may be of valley construction—that is, built as two small pitched roofs which meet each other—and the valley gutter where they meet may have deteriorated, letting in damp. Broken or cracked parapets and copings on roofs, balconies and facades will indicate possible penetration by rain. Flat roofs to extensions, porches, bay windows, balconies, may have coverings of lead, zinc, asphalt or copper which have worn, cracked, split or bubbled over the years, letting moisture in.

Inside the house, damaged wallpaper at skirting level is a sign of rising damp. After a long period of dry weather the clue may be a faint water mark on the wall. Spots of damp, as distinct from areas of damp, are signs that when the house was being built careless bricklayers let mortar drop on to the metal ties which bind the two skins of a cavity wall together and damp has crept across and penetrated the inner brick skin.

Damage higher up in a room, or in the upper parts of a house, seen on the inside of an exterior wall, suggests damp getting in through defective flashings, cracked lintels, old pointing, vertical tiling or too thin a skin of bricks exposed to driving rain. Ceiling stains indicate penetration through roofs, through broken copings or through broken parapets. Stains on walls at the top or sides of window frames indicate penetration of damp round the frames, possibly through failure of dampproof courses.

Is there rot in the house?

Rot is the beastly daughter of sneaky damp. When moisture penetrates wood wet rot sets in. If the spot is unventilated dry rot prevails. Rot may be quite hidden and undetectable to your amateur inspection, as in the joists under a flat roof; or be relatively hard to detect, as in an upper floor where joists have become rotted through damp penetrating a thin skin wall much exposed to rain, or in the floor under a lavatory where a cracked bowl or leaking waste pipe has been letting water seep and spread under the boards.

Dry rot has a musty smell which you may recognise. If the outbreak is not insidious you may detect it, in a skirting say or in floorboards, by a kind of crazing in the surface of the wood. Use your screwdriver first to tap the wood and then if the tone sounds dull rather than ringing and firm dig with the sharp end into the board: if the wood has a cork-like texture and crumbles it is rotted.

Sagging floors may be a sign of rot, the floor joists being susceptible to damp where they rest on the wall plate—a horizontal timber support fastened to the inside of an external wall. If the ground floor of the house is a suspended one—that is, floorboards laid on joists supported by diminutive sleeper walls— and it has a lot of give when you jump up and down on it, that is a clue to rot being below.

You should look for woodworm and other beetle infestation. New looking holes in wood are a sign that the pest is active: so are piles of clean looking dust near the holes.

If new floorboards have been laid you should ask why. Sometimes sound floorboards are laid over unsound ones as a quick and cheap expedient to get the house sold, and if you see that floorboards abut the skirting instead of passing underneath it you should be suspicious.

The odds are about four to one that if the house is more than 35 years old you *will* find woodworm and wet rot damage. Putting things to rights is not cheap: the average cost (1967 figures) of remedial treatment in houses built between 1900 and 1909 is £90; in houses built between 1930 and 1939 about £70. Curing of dry rot is even more expensive: for the older group of houses the average cost of cure is £200: for the more recent houses £150.

A case of contradictory reports

If you see signs of beetle infestation you will probably call in one of the firms who specialise in eradicating the pest and treating timbers against further outbreaks. Such firms will, without charge, make a detailed inspection of the house to look specifically for infestation but although this is a useful thing and has a comforting ring about it here is a story to make you think. It concerns a house in west London, the time 1967. The house was in process of being sold and the buyer's surveyor had noticed signs of woodworm and advised that a specialist firm be consulted.

The buyer accordingly got in touch with a well-known firm and asked them to inspect and report. By mistake the firm sent two of its men to make different inspections at different times: the mistake was not realised and so in due course the buyer received two separate reports, one in the first post and the other in the midday post. He was surprised to see that the first report said that in the attic there was no need for treatment but that the second report said that full treatment should be carried out; and that the first report said that the timbers of the floor in the rear bedroom could not be inspected because of furniture and carpeting, but the second report said that the timbers in this floor needed full treatment. The matter was resolved by the two men making a joint inspection all over again under the flinty eyes of the firm's regional manager, with the buyer being present to make sure for himself that this time their report would accord with realities.

Next—Is the house standing up straight?

See if there is settlement or distortion of the structure. Every house settles after it is built but some settle more than others and some go on settling.

Clay subsoil is a troublemaker on this count. Clay expands in rain and shrinks in dry weather, and if there is not a sound continuous covering skin of paving or concrete round the house the movement can be excessive. For this reason clay subsoil is less of a hazard in towns than in the country. On a slope, clay has a tendency to creep downhill, as it were, taking the foundations with it. Poplar trees can be pernicious near houses built on clay, taking a great amount of moisture from the soil and causing extreme drying out.

Foundations may settle unevenly in any subsoil. There may be a half cellar under the house, so that the foundations on the cellar side go much deeper than those under the other walls—the result being that the house settles on the side of the shallower founds. Foundations may be simply inadequate. Old houses built on chalk or well compacted subsoil may have none at all.

Tree roots can damage the foundations of a house, bringing about settlement, and defective drains running under a house can cause internal settlement.

Settlement is indicated, on the outside of a house, by window frames being out of horizontal, lines of bricks sagging or running down one way, cracks, tilting arches. Inside, the clues are door and window frames out of true; cracks (not hair cracks or little cracks, which are usually not serious: probe cracks with a thin long blade and if the blade goes in a long way you will know what to think), especially cracks running from the corners of frames or where wall meets wall or ceiling meets wall; cracked hearths in upper floors; and sloping floors.

Floors sloping inwards indicate internal settlement, naturally; and you should know that settlement, or the signs of it, may be produced by or be associated with the effects of downwards and outwards pressures by the roof. If the roof is partly supported by an internal wall any weakening of the wall—perhaps brought about by the opening up of separated rooms below, or excessive weight having been placed on the floors which it supports—will result in settlement, the signs of which will be cracks and distorted frames.

If the roof was badly constructed outwards pressure may cause exterior walls to bulge, particularly at weak points between windows. Bulging walls may be serious defects or simply harmless evidence of old age. You can detect bulges if they are not obvious by squinting along the line of the wall, comparing it if possible with a true vertical in a new building near by.

A bulge in a gable wall, which is not placed to be affected by outwards roof thrust, may be due to there being little or no horizontal restraint from joists, or to joists having been weakened through rot. Whatever the cause, serious bulging may mean that a section of the wall must be rebuilt. Like putting to rights a roof sagging on timbers long since due for renewal, the work will be expensive and you may well decide that it is better to go and look at another house than take on that kind of liability.

Other sources of trouble and danger

You must look for odd sources of trouble in and around the house:

Check all window fastenings and external locks.

If the house is empty find the stopcock, turn the water on and make a round of the taps, turning them on. If the flow of water is slow the pipes are probably furred up. Check all piping in view and then go round again looking for leaks in basins, in sinks and at wastepipe joints.

Check the plumbing for noisiness.

Lead water pipes may be sagging unsupported for long runs, and in remote places may be leaking from pinholes caused by the action of lime.

Unlagged long lengths of hot water piping mean considerable heat loss. Lengths of piping, for hot or cold water, unlagged and close to exterior walls are at risk from frost. So are water tanks so placed. So are extended runs of waste pipes on the outside walls of the house.

If the electric wiring is more than 20 years old it will probably have to be replaced. Two points: metal domed switches are positively dangerous and so are two-pin power points. The electricity board will refuse to reconnect for you if they think the system defective. Rewiring is a quite expensive operation at about £5 a point.

If fireplaces have been blocked up, ventilating grilles should have been put in the coverings. If this has not been done the chimney flues will be unaired and be prone to damp.

Slipped tiles on the roof or evidence of recent new fastenings for tiles are clues that the tiles are decayed or that the nails have rusted and that retiling is due.

Bulges in ceilings may indicate leaks, or that the plaster key is no longer holding to laths.

Galvanized cold water tanks do not have a life much longer than 15 years and so you should check the tank, which is probably in the attic, for disintegration through rust. If the hatch to the attic is too small to let a new tank in this is a severe disadvantage.

Look at tall pipes on the outside of the house: rust may be making them inherently dangerous or weakening the brackets. If the chimney is leaning it may be dangerous and may have to be taken down or rebuilt.

Airbricks in the outer walls near the ground may be blocked up, covered by heaped-up garden soil, or be absent altogether. Airbricks are important because they allow air to circulate under floors and so prevent rot.

Trees near the house may represent a danger, through spread of roots damaging the foundations of the house and the houses of neighbours, and damaging drains.

CHAPTER FOUR

WHERE TO GET A MORTGAGE

WE HAVE ALREADY MENTIONED mortgages many times in *Chapters 1 and 2* and we know that by 'mortgage' we mean a loan which enables an ordinary person to buy a house which he couldn't possibly afford to pay for in a lump sum out of his own resources. It is surprising how many different kinds of mortgage schemes there are and we will be looking at them in detail in *Chapter 6*. But for the moment, why is the arrangement called a 'mortgage'? The word is used because the house is mortgaged to the lender, who keeps the title deeds* in his possession to ensure that the borrower does not quietly sell up and disappear without paying him back; or that if the borrower fails to keep up the repayments the lender can sell the house and get his money back that way.

If you are buying a house for the first time the main thing you will be concerned about is getting as big a mortgage as possible and having the repayments spread over a long period. This will be discussed partly in this section and in more detail in *Chapter 5*, but the main question at this stage is 'Where can you *get* a mortgage?' When you have briefed yourself on that you can begin to think about the ins and outs of particular mortgage arrangements.

You should have some understanding of the mortgage market and how different lenders operate. That word 'market' is an apt one. Visualise the whole of Britain as a market place with dotted here and there, in its towns and cities, hundreds and thousands of money shops all offering mortgages. You may wonder where they all get their money from, and the fact is that sometimes their sources of money are ample and then mortgages are easy to get and sometimes the sources dry up and then mortgages are hard to get. But if you know your way around it will be easier to get a mortgage even in difficult times when money generally is in short supply.

A council mortgage is best if you can get it

There are three main kinds of mortgage shop. The one where you may expect the best deal, if you can get it, is your town hall or county hall.

---

* *See Glossary.*

Local councils can and do lend money for house purchase and have been doing so for a long while. More than a thousand councils have lending schemes, and that is most of them. Councils are not in the mortgages business for the sake of the business itself but for the sake of discharging part of their responsibility to see that people are properly housed. It follows that they will lend tolerantly and favourably when they can.

'When they can . . .' Council lending funds have not always been considerable, and in the past they have been subject to sudden cutting back, as happened by Treasury decree at the beginning of 1969. However, the Government has since lifted the ceiling on council lending, and so there is every good reason for making your first step in a quest for a mortgage a call or letter to the clerk of your local council or corporation.* Note that your chance of a council mortgage may be better towards the end of the financial year because after Christmas there is a reallocation of mortgage funds among councils and those funds have to be used up before March 31.

If your council shop is open and in business, so to speak, and you are accepted as a customer you should find that you can get a mortgage rather more easily than from another kind of lender for the purchase of a leasehold house (*see Chapter 7*), for the purchase of a flat or maisonette (*see Chapter 8*), or for an old house.

The terms of the loan are likely to be better also. Loans of 100 per cent are more common from councils, and it is not unknown for repayments to be arranged over 40 years. Your mortgage rating may be put higher, with overtime, wife's earnings and general family earnings taken more generously into account. Also valuation (*see Chapter 1, page 14*) may be more favourable and, as with mortgages from other lenders, loan percentage may be increased through a mortgage indemnity arrangement (*see Chapter 2, page 22; and Chapter 5, page 59*), possibly at no charge.

Councils, like some building societies, operate the 100 per cent mortgages scheme and the option mortgage scheme (*see Chapter 5, pages 65 and 60*); and, as may be arranged with mortgages from other sources, a council mortgage may be linked with endowment insurance (*see Chapter 6, page 75*). Councils can lend money for the building of a new house (*see Chapter 10*)

---

* *Or the town development corporation for a house in a New Town: or the Commission for New Towns.* See Chapter 1, page 20.

Who to go to in the mortgage market

LENDERS			BORROWERS	BEST WAYS TO BORROW
Local Authority Maximum price £5000	Building Society Maximum price £7500–£10000	Insurance Co. Maximum price up to £25000		
●			Buying in overspill area or new town	⎫
●	○		Buying leasehold; short lease	⎪
●	○		Buying an old house	⎬ Ordinary mortgage
●	○		Buying a flat or maisonette	⎪
●	○		Financing a housing association	⎭
●	●		Modest income, little savings	Hundred per cent mortgage under Government scheme, linked with option mortgage subsidy.
●	●		Some savings or collateral, middling income, not paying much tax	Ordinary mortgage; consider opting for option mortgage subsidy.
●	●	●	Savings in hand or collateral, good income, steady prospects. Paying much tax at standard rate	Endowment (or equity-linked) mortgage: or mixed policy mortgage
●	●	●	Good income, paying much tax at standard rate—expectation of windfall in future	Interest-only mortgage; or half repayment mortgage
	●	●	Savings in hand or collateral, steady prospects, wife working	Young married couple's mortgage (joint income mortgage)
	●	●	Substantial savings or collateral, good income, paying much tax at standard or surtax rate	Endowment (or equity-linked) mortgage
Housing Corporation & Building Society			Financing a co-ownership housing society	Endowment (or equity-linked) mortgage

KEY ◯ less favourable

and for housing group schemes (*see Chapter 11*).

You need not confine your inquiries to the council of your district. You may also look to the council in the district where you work or in a district where you intend to move. Nor will a council's mortgage scheme necessarily be restricted to the purchase of a house locally: you may be able to borrow the money to buy or build somewhere else. In Lewisham in south-east London in late 1969 mortgages (100 per cent in this case) were offered to outsiders to buy homes within the council's district.

This may all seem too good to be true, but you must always bear in mind that supply of money to councils is not nearly as great as to the other kinds of lenders, and that other factors too may reduce your chance of getting a council mortgage.

You may find that priority is given to people of low income; to council tenants; to people who are losing their present homes through redevelopment or slum clearance; to the homeless, those poorly housed or overcrowded; to residents moving to New Towns or overspill areas to buy houses there; to engaged couples or the newly married (*see chart*).

You may find that a council's interest rate* on its mortgages is high. Five per cent of the councils who operate mortgage schemes charge $10\frac{1}{2}$ per cent because they cannot get the money themselves much cheaper. Ealing, in west London, put its rate at $9\frac{3}{4}$ per cent in October, 1969, Lewisham's rate was put at $9\frac{1}{2}$ per cent about the same time, the rate in the London borough of Harringey is $9\frac{7}{8}$ per cent.

Council mortgages generally take longer to arrange than other kinds, and most councils refuse to give mortgages for houses costing above a certain level. You may also find that your council will lend only to people who have failed to get a mortgage anywhere else, regarding itself as a lender of last resort. However, note that a local council is never quite that, as if you get a refusal there you may then try your county council for a loan.

A building society mortgage is the most usual

The second kind of mortgage shop are the building societies. 'Second', of course, does not mean second in importance. In 1970 the building societies lent £1986 million to housebuyers, almost eclipsing the councils and also putting the insurance companies (the third main source of house loans) very much in the shade. In fact the odds are that you will end up with a mortgage from a

---

* *See Glossary.*

building society.

You can note that the best deal for the not very well off person comes from the margin of building society operations where public money is injected into the system. The option mortgage scheme (*see Chapter 5, page 60*) has had the effect of increasing the amount that low-income people can borrow or alternatively of reducing the deposit they have to put down. Building societies have also accepted the principle of 100 per cent mortgages linked with the option mortgage scheme (*see Chapter 5, page 65*).

How do you set about finding a building society who will make you a loan? That's rather like asking a man watching the Miss World contest on television which of the girls he'd like to take out to dinner and so on. However strong his interest he would answer shortly that he wouldn't know how to begin. It is possible to write to all of the building societies listed in the *Building Societies Year Book* which you will find at your public library, but there are about 550 all told and the task would be overwhelming. A list, with addresses, of the 20 leading societies and some other smaller ones is given at the end of this section, and this will offer you a practicable start. You may have a society local to your district. A bank manager, solicitor, accountant, estate agent may recommend one to you, or you may know of one through parents, relatives, or friends. A very remote chance, your firm may run its own building society, as does the John Summers steelworks in faraway Flintshire. Or you may consult a broker (*this Chapter, page 49*).

You should equip yourself with a good understanding of the rules that building societies in general apply in granting or refusing requests for mortgages. The key to building society thinking is caution above all in lending money for house purchase, even against the security of a sound house which could be sold easily if the mortgage arrangement broke down. This is the main reason for a building society valuation often proving lower than price, and the mortgage offer being only a percentage of the valuation figure somewhat below the full amount. A building society considers that it is putting its money at risk in making a loan, and as it is accountable to shareholders and investors, it will try to keep the supposed risk as low as possible. You will be beginning to see the fundamental reason for building society lending policy having to be more stringent than councils'.

A building society will want to know your job and salary and will ask for two or more references, including one from your employer. It will like you best as a borrower if you are young, a professional man or in a secure job like teaching, the Civil

Service, the police force; less if you are middle-aged or elderly, a window cleaner, gardener, salesman on commission, building worker, journalist, artist, small antiques dealer, musician, actor.

If you are self-employed you will be asked to produce accounts showing steady and reasonable income in recent years.

If you are a woman you will be favoured for a mortgage if you are over 40 (but not too much so), if you are professionally qualified or are a teacher or nurse; at the least you must be in a regular job which is going to continue (*see also Chapter 5*).

A building society will not let you commit yourself to repayments higher than it thinks you can reasonably afford (the rules on this are explained in *Chapter 5, page 56*). Building society loans are generally limited to houses not costing more than £10,000 and in practice the maximum is usually set at £7500.

From all the many different customers who come to the building societies for mortgages about half a million are fixed up every year, and so clearly a person's chances are good for all the apparent rigorousness of the system. There are indications that lending policy is being liberalised, if slowly. Public and Government pressure is obliging the societies to reconsider their traditional practices, and consequently it is well worth directing your mortgage inquiries to a number of societies in the hope of finding one or two who will be more than usually helpful. You don't have to be rich to get a mortgage.

Here is some information about particular building societies which may be of help to you. Two of the big societies—the Nationwide and the Alliance—say that they grant high-percentage loans, up to 95 per cent, over 30-year and 35-year repayment terms. The Nationwide also favours housing groups (*see Chapter 11*). The Halifax is better than some others in lending on older houses. So are the Chelsea and South London, and the Property Owners Building Society, both of whom are also helpful with the purchase of old houses for modernisation (*see Chapter 9*). The Abbey National has a good record in lending on older houses, the Woolwich Equitable is tolerant to young people not very well off, the Leicester Permanent makes loans over longer terms than average, as does the Anglia. The Burnely lends on flats (*see Chapter 8*) produced by conversions. The Lambeth operates a 'young married couples' mortgage scheme which takes wife's earnings into account: so does the City and Metropolitan (*see also Chapter 6, page 72*). City and Metropolitan also operates a

---

*See Glossary.

mortgage scheme which takes account of future regular salary increments (*see Chapter 6, page 73*). The Guardian will take half a wife's income into account, the Bromley will take a quarter of wife's income into account. The Abbey National operates a 'half repayment' mortgage scheme and 'interest only' mortgage schemes (*see Chapter 6, page 73*), although the usefulness of these is limited to a few borrowers as apart from anything else they are only offered up to 66 per cent.

It is often said that you stand a better chance of a mortgage with a particular society if you have been saving with the society, but experience sometimes contradicts this. However, if you are able to plan six months or a year ahead it may be a good idea to put your savings with a recommended building society in advance of your mortgage application. The societies have been urged by the Government to grant mortgages readily to people who save with them for six months at a rate equal to the eventual repayments on a mortgage. Additionally, a scheme, Save As You Earn, makes long-term saving with a society more attractive. The saver contracts to put a sum, maximum £20 a month, into a society month by month for five years. If he keeps to his side of the bargain, he gets a bonus equivalent to a year's savings, free of tax. If he maintains the contract for a further two years the bonus is doubled.

An insurance company mortgage is generally for better-off people

Insurance companies are the third main source of mortgages. A number of insurance companies lend money to the general public (as distinct from existing policy-holders) for house purchase and these companies too are listed at the end of this section.

Their approach is generally similar to that of the building societies, except that they are often more willing to give mortgages for flats. Their requirements as to borrower's income approximate to those of the building societies, although they do give higher percentage loans and borrowing periods may be longer. In giving you a mortgage an insurance company naturally will be interested in linking the arrangement with an insurance policy of one kind or another; so that borrowing from the insurance company field is practicable only if your income enables you to keep up an insurance policy as well as repay the mortgage.

Insurance companies range to higher prices than the building societies—say £12,500, £15,000, £20,000, £25,000.

You can employ a broker to negotiate a mortgage for you

Brokers are people who are specialists in arranging house

purchase finance. On the face of it this is a useful service but the trouble is that mortgage broking is not an organised profession. Anyone can set himself up as a mortgage broker, and so there is a risk of clients being charged for poor service, or paying fees and yet end up with no mortgage, or committing themselves to a mortgage arrangement which is unfavourable to them or is really beyond what they can afford.

Here is a story to make you think. Mr Devlin Ruddock wanted to raise a mortgage of £4500 to buy a house at Thornton Heath, Surrey. He paid a broker a fee of £75 and after a while was told that an arrangement could be made whereby £3000 would be advanced by a building society and £500 by a merchant bank. The remaining £1000 he needed, it was suggested, could be arranged for an extra fee of £11 and an undertaking to pay a perpetual rent of £3 a week which would be binding on subsequent owners of the house. Mr Ruddock had the good sense to reject this extortionate arrangement and demand his money back, and after a while fortunately got it.

This unpleasant story stands as a warning, and even though Mr Ruddock's experience was extreme rather than typical it serves to make the point that using a broker may be either not much help or not nearly as helpful as you may hope and expect. This may seem heavily critical, but housebuying in Britain is still largely an unprotected consumer activity and mortgage brokering is possibly the least regulated part of it. Of course there are very many reputable, expert and genuinely helpful brokers and brokering firms. If you do go to a broker follow these rules:

Ask for an agreement in writing which states the mortgage you are asking the broker to arrange for you and the fee you will pay him if he is successful.

Don't sign any commitment on your side and pay no fee until the broker shows you a written offer of the sort of mortgage you want, on suitable terms. Compare the terms of any such offer, especially interest rate,* with what building societies are offering generally, and if the terms seem abnormal or unreasonable reject them.

Pay no fee if no suitable mortgage arrangement is forth-

* *See Glossary.*

coming. If the broker initially asks for a promise that you will pay him a fee if the negotiations for a mortage for you have to be broken off through no fault of his weigh this up carefully and in any event do not commit yourself to a higher payment than 10 guineas in such circumstances.

A broker's earnings for getting you a suitable mortgage should not exceed £21 or 2 per cent of the mortgage, whichever is the higher figure. If his negotiations include arranging an endowment insurance policy (*see Chapter 6, page 75*), linked with your mortgage he will get a commission from the insurance company and this should be deducted from the £21 figure to reach any fee payable by you. Good brokers are content with the commission alone in such a case and charge the client no fee.

Because brokers often rely mainly for their earnings on insurance commission you must be careful about being persuaded to take on an insurance arrangement associated with the mortgage. It may not be necessary and it may be more than you can afford. On the other hand it may be in your interests to take out an endowment mortgage (*see Chapter 6, page 75*), or your inquiries may incline you to think that it is an appropriate thing for you to do in your circumstances; in which case you can be very positively helped by the advice of a good insurance broker. This may seem contradictory after the warnings given above; but it is not, because the warnings apply to dealings with a broker whose main help to you you hope will be the securing of a mortgage. Going to an insurance broker for expert advice on insurance associated with housebuying is rather different, but of course even then you must be businesslike over fees, agreements and so on.

A broker may ask you to hand over to him the building society's valuation fee (*see Chapter 1, page 14*). If you do pass the money over ask for evidence that the fee has in fact been passed on to the building society—the society's receipt or letter of acknowledgement. Be similarly cautious over any sums a broker may ask you to hand to him on any other account.

Never be persuaded to a 'second mortgage' arrangement being negotiated on your behalf to help you buy a house.

As far as the ordinary first-time housebuyer is concerned second mortgages are what their name might convey—second class propositions involving high interest rates,* short repayment periods, and heavy real cost (*see also Chapter 5*). Second mortgages emanate from the finance market outside the sober and well-regulated territory of the building societies and insurance companies, and they are best left well alone.

As suggested earlier, the warnings given with regard to broker services need not deter you from using a broker to find a mortgage for you. The best brokers are undoubtedly expert at raising mortgage funds and in advising you over terms, and it is a fact that building societies do give some brokers mortgage quotas for their clients. Many brokerages are large and well established and thoroughly reputable business concerns. Some charge no fees at all. But there are hundreds who operate less scrupulously, and so you must be careful.

If you can, deal with a broker who is a member of the Corporation of Insurance Brokers, 15 St Helen's Place, London EC3, or the Association of Insurance Brokers, Craven House, 121 Kingsway, London WC2. You can get lists of their members by writing to those addresses.

Note also that a Corporation of Mortgage Brokers has been established, registered as a limited company, with the aim of regulating mortgage brokers. You can get a list of the member brokers of this organisation from 6a The Forbury, Reading, Berks.

You may get a mortgage from other sources

There are a few other sources your bank, solicitor or broker may be able to tap for you—trustee funds, friendly societies and welfare-orientated organisations like RAFA and other ex-Service bodies. A builder or developer may have access to mortgage funds to enable you to buy one of his houses.

You may have the offer of a personal loan and if you have and you accept it it is as well to have the arrangement set out in a formal agreement. Your employer may also lend you the money to buy a house but you might regret accepting it later on when you want to change jobs.

* *See Glossary.*

You may be offered a private mortgage

This possibility is often mentioned in advice literature to house-buyers but it is hard to find a case quoted. Here is one now.

Mr and Mrs Barry Bailey were interested in buying a two-bedroom bungalow, Sherwood, at Three Bridges in Sussex. The price was £3850 but the best mortgage offer they could get from a building society was 80 per cent, which seemed to put the chance out of their reach because deposit and costs would have come to about £800 which was more than they had.

However, the owner, a woman, suggested a private mortgage. The terms would be £300 down and another £100 in a year's time, with the balance to be paid over 20 years at a fixed interest rate of 6 per cent. The Baileys could at any time make extra payments in multiples of £10 to reduce the debt the quicker.

On these reasonable terms the couple got their bungalow.

The arrangement included a feature which is not uncommon with private mortgages. The seller was liable to tax on the interest the Baileys would be paying her. She suggested, and they concurred, that every six months they give her a sum over and above the agreed repayments to cover her tax liability. The sum was about £50, not a high figure, and since the seller was concerned only to soften her tax commitment, not charge the Baileys more, she deducted the £50 payments from their outstanding debt to her, with the effect that the repayment period was shortened to about 14 years.

The story usefully shows how a private mortgage may be arranged where an owner is not pressed for an immediate full cash return on the house he is selling. On the same basis, an owner may agree to a private mortgage arrangement covering part of the purchase price, say £300 or £500, to enable the buyer to go ahead with the deal. In such a case it would probably happen that the sum involved has to be paid to the owner over a comparatively short period, say five years, and the buyer would have to decide whether he could afford the extra sum in addition to his repayments on the mortgage under which he has raised the bulk of the purchase price. If you are offered such a private mortgage you should pay special attention to two points: 1 That the interest rate is reasonable and that the interest is charged on the reducing sum not on the whole sum throughout the whole period; and 2 That the seller does not reserve the right to call in the loan at short notice.

You should check the terms of any mortgage you are offered

You may be so glad to get a mortgage offer that you will not want to question the terms of the loan. That is up to you, but the sensible thing is to examine the lender's terms critically even if you have no choice but to accept, paying particular attention to penalties attached to repaying the loan early (known as redemption charges*), the cost of any mortgage protection arrangement (*see Chapter 6, page 79*), and if the mortgage is an endowment mortgage (*see Chapter 6, page 75*), whether the terms and bonus expectations are as favourable with an insurance company nominated by the lender as they would be from some other company you can go to assuming you have free choice.

The leading 20 building societies

Halifax, Permanent Buildings, Halifax, Yorks.
Hastings and Thanet, Thrift House, Collington Avenue, Bexhill, Sussex
Abbey National, Abbey House, Baker Street, London W1
Nationwide, New Oxford House, High Holborn, London WC1
Temperance Permanent, 223–227 Regent Street, London W1
Woolwich Equitable, Equitable House, Woolwich, London SE18
Cheltenham and Gloucester, 37–43 Clarence Street, Cheltenham, Glos.
Leeds Permanent, Permanent House, The Headrow, Leeds 1
Bristol and West, Broad Quay, Bristol 1
Alliance, Alliance House, Hove Park, Hove, Sussex
Northern Rock, Market Street, Newcastle on Tyne 1
Pronvincial, Provincial House, Market Street, Bradford, Yorks.
Huddersfield, Britannia Buildings, Huddersfield, Yorks.
Leek and Westbourne, New Stockwell House, Leek, Staffs.
Bradford Permanent, 57–63 Sunbridge Road, Bradford 1
Leicester Permanent, Oadby, Leics.
Leicester Temperance, Halford House, Charles Street, Leicester
Bradford and Bingley, POB 2, Bingley, Yorks.
Anglia, Abington Street, Northampton
Burnley, Grimshaw Street, Burnley, Lancs.

Other building societies mentioned in this section

Bromley, 182 High Street, Bromley, Kent   BRI 1HE
Lambeth, 118–120 Westminster Bridge Road, London SE1
City and Metropolitan, 145 Moorgate, London EC2
Guardian, Guardian House, 120 High Holborn, London WC1

---

* *See Glossary.*

Insurance companies who advance mortgages to the general public*

Provident Life Association of London Ltd., 246 Bishopsgate, London EC2

Scottish Amicable Life Assurance Society, 35 St. Vincent Place, Glasgow C1

Scottish Life Assurance Company Ltd., 19 St Andrew Square, Edinburgh 2

Scottish Mutual Assurance Society, 109 St. Vincent Street, Glasgow C2

Scottish Equitable, 28 St. Andrew Square, Edinburgh 2

Scottish Provident Institution, 6 St Andrew Square, Edinburgh 2

Sentinel Insurance Co. Ltd., 11–13 Holborn Viaduct, London EC1

Standard Life Assurance Co., 3 St. George Street, Edinburgh 2

Sun Life Assurance Society Ltd., 107 Cheapside, London EC2

United Friendly Insurance Co. Ltd., 42 Southwark Bridge Road, London SE1

University Life Assurance Society, 4 Coleman Street, London EC2

Welfare Insurance Co., 35–37 Cannon Street, London EC4

British National Life Insurance Society Ltd., Spencer House, 4 South Place, London EC2

Coronet Insurance Co. Ltd., Fountain House, 130 Fenchurch Street, London EC3

Equitable Life Assurance Society, 4 Coleman Street, London EC2

Friends Provident and Century Group, 7 Leadenhall Street, London EC2

Gresham Life Assurance Society Ltd., 59 Gresham Street, London EC2

Hodge Life Assurance Co. Ltd., 30 Windsor Place, Cardiff

Life, Casualty and General Insurance Co. Ltd., Argyle House, Joel Street, Northwood Hills, Middlesex

London Life Association Ltd., 81 King William Street, London EC4

National Mutual Life Assurance Society, 5 Bow Churchyard, London EC4

National Provident Institution, 48 Gracechurch Street, London EC3

Noble Lowndes Annuities Ltd., NLA House, Lansdowne Road, Croydon, Surrey

Norwich Union Life Insurance Society, POB 4, Norwich   NOR 88A

Pioneer Life Assurance Co. Ltd., 31 Dale Street, Liverpool 1

---

* *With acknowledgements to the Life Offices' Association.*

CHAPTER FIVE

HOW BIG A MORTGAGE CAN YOU GET?

WHEN YOU BUY A HOUSE you finance the purchase in two big steps. The first is to contribute out of your savings a proportion of the price: this contribution from you is your down payment or deposit*, and most people find it the biggest barrier in the way of achieving their ambition of house purchase.

The second step is to borrow the remainder of the purchase price on mortgage, undertaking to repay the loan, with interest, over an extended period like 20 or 25 years.

It's obvious that the bigger the percentage loan you can obtain the lower will be the contribution, the deposit, you have to find out of your cash resources.

How big a mortgage can you get?

It depends partly on whether you are young or not so young. The question of age apart, the two main considerations are your income and your status.

Let's take income first

Building societies have two ways of calculating how big a mortgage they will grant in relation to your income. The first is the two and a half times earning rule. Take your yearly income, the gross figure (that is the amount you earn before deductions) and multiply it by 2·5. The result is the mortgage figure. Thus if you earn £1200 a year you qualify for a mortgage of £3000.

The second is the monthly income rule. Take your monthly income and divide by four. The resulting figure is the maximum you will be allowed to commit yourself to in monthly outgoings as a houseowner. Thus if your monthly income is £100 you will not be allowed to take on commitments of more than £25 a month. Let's say that your rates† as a houseowner will be £4 a month:

---

* We have already used the term 'deposit' twice in this book and here we are using it in a third connection. 1 There is 'deposit to stakeholder (page 13); 2 there is 10 per cent deposit handed over to the seller at exchange of contracts (page 24); and 3 there is 'deposit' in the sense of buyer's total cash contribution towards purchase price (this page). It is really quite coherent. The first deposit is carried forward to be included in the second and the combined sum is then carried forward to make up, or part make up, buyer's total contribution towards purchase price.
† See Glossary.

that leaves £21 as the maximum you may commit yourself to in mortgage repayments. On this basis you qualify for a mortgage of £2800, assuming the loan is at $8\frac{1}{2}$ per cent and the mortgage period is 25 years.

You will see that under the first formula you rate for a bigger loan than under the second. Earning £1200 a year (£100 a month), you would get a loan of £3000 under the first formula but only £2800 under the second. There is no knowing which formula will be applied until you have approached a building society. But it is wise to regard the two and a half times rule as a working maximum and the other rule as the more realistic one.

Sometimes the first rule may be stretched to allow a loan of three times yearly income, but this is not common. In London, where house prices are very high, such stretching may be tolerated as necessary, but not as a rule elsewhere.

Now let's look at the status factor

Status, when it comes to housebuying, is nothing to do with your show of worldly wealth, having a bigger car than your friends, or carrying a credit card. It is what you are judged to be worth in terms of regular and reliable repaying of a mortgage. Consequently it pertains to your salary partially, but perhaps more essentially to the security of your job and your prospects in it; your married or ex-married state; the number of children you have to support or the number you may be expected to have; and your sex.

You will remember that we touched on this in *Chapter 4*. If you are a professional person, a policeman, council employee, computer programmer, teacher—for example—your job status is good in a building society's eyes. If you are a farmworker, a waiter, a self-employed artisan, a salesman on commission, your job status is not very high.

As we have noted, if you are a woman your rating is high if you are professionally qualified, good if you are a teacher or an established nurse. It is lower if you are a clippie, typist, telephonist, receptionist. It is improved if you are over 40 (but not too much so: remember the age factor), detracted from if you are younger and consequently more liable to have children. Of course this consideration mainly applies to cases of couples applying for mortgages: it has yet to be reported that evidence of sterilisation has been offered to and accepted by a building society as improving status but undoubtedly in this age of vasectomics and tubal ligations it will come.

Here is a picture of a high-status borrower as a building

society would draw it. He is 26, married, has two children and intends to have no more, earns about £2000 a year in the Civil Service, and is seeking a loan of £5000 to buy a three-bedroom semi-detached house with garage on a modern estate developed by a reliable builder under National House Builders Registration Council* guarantee near shops, good schools and bus routes and close to a railway station giving a quick journey into town. The further you depart from the standards set by this paragon the less favourable the mortgage arrangement you can hope for.

This may seem somewhat discouraging, but of course very few people do accord to the ideal standard yet most get mortgages. There are a number of ways by which you may be able to stretch your rating, so to put it, to get a bigger mortgage than at first sight you seem entitled to, and we will be looking at them in a moment. First, however, let us get this question of the buyer's cash contribution, or deposit, quite clear.

Advertisements directed at housebuyers often suggest that five per cent of purchase price is all you need to contribute towards the cost of a house, but these suggestions are downright misleading. As we have noted earlier in this book, building society practice is to offer about 80 per cent of valuation or price whichever is the lower, and the reality is (1970 figures) the average loan on new houses of an average price of £4590 is 74 per cent and on not-new houses of an average price of £4484 is 69·6 per cent. It has been estimated that 60 per cent of brorowers contribute deposits of more than £600, the average deposit is about £1230, and the average loan £3725.

Why do building societies so restrict their loans and insist on such substantial cash deposits? One reason is that they are reluctant to carry all of the supposed risk of sinking a sum of money in the purchase of a house. Another reason is that by restricting the size of individual loans the societies are able to spread their funds over a higher number of borrowers. A third reason is that the system encourages thrift. Another is that when a borrower has a good deal of his own capital tied up in a house this helps ensure that he will take an interest in the property and keep it well maintained. However, it is probably the 'risk' reason which is the dominant one and it follows that you may improve your mortgage rating if you can give a building society an assurance of one kind or another that the 'risk' is less than normal.

---

* *See Glossary.*

You may get a better rating if you can quote a guarantor

You may know of someone who has money invested in some sound quarter—perhaps in trustee funds or with the building societies themselves. If such a person will stand guarantor for you you may be better placed for a loan when otherwise your application might be regarded as having only a marginal chance: in other words, by producing a suitable guarantor you may improve your status in a building society's eyes. Over and above this, a guarantee by someone who actually holds shares in the society from whom you will be borrowing may well put you in line for a bigger mortgage rather than just 'propping up' your application. Note that your employer may be acceptable as a guarantor. Further, if you are elderly, a guarantee from your children, or other younger relatives, may put you in line for a mortgage.

You can get a bigger mortgage if you offer collateral

Collateral is another word for 'security' and security is what building societies prize above all.

If you have an insurance policy with a surrender value you may offer this as collateral.

If you have shares or savings certificates or holdings of Government securities you may offer these as collateral.

If your parents, or relatives, have a house not fully mortgaged —that is, partly or wholly paid for—the value of the paid-for part may be accepted as collateral by a building society.

You can get a bigger mortgage through a mortgage indemnity arrangement

We have seen how such an arrangement worked in the case of the Hunters (*see Chapter 2, page 22*). Few borrowers resist such a proposal when it is made by a building society. The mortgage offer may be increased to 85, 90, or 95 per cent under the arrangement which, you will remember, involves the borrower paying for an insurance policy under which the building society will be reimbursed by the insurance company if something goes wrong with the mortgage arrangement later on and it is faced with the loss of some of its money.

The arrangement is called mortgage indemnity as a rule, but other terms for it are mortgage guarantee, excess advance charge, and hedging policy. Its attraction to borrowers is that apart from their being relieved of the need to find a larger deposit it is usually arranged for the cost of the policy, a once and once only premium, to be paid by the building society and added to the loan.

The charge for a mortgage indemnity policy is usually £4·50 for every extra £100 the building society lends you above its original offer, this rate applying to mortgage arrangements where the repayment period is more than 20 years. The rate may be higher—one building society arrangement involves payment of £7.50 for every extra £100; or it may be lower—as with the Civil Service Housing Association in relation to mortgages arranged with the Civil Service Building Society, when the rate is £3 for every excess £100. On an option mortgage arrangement (see later) the rate is £2·50 for every extra £100 lent for a period up to 20 years, £3·50 for every extra £100 lent for a longer period than that. It is also possible for a mortgage indemnity to be arranged involving jointly the Government, a local authority and the building society, but this scheme although cheaper than the commercial schemes seems to be hardly ever used.

You can get a bigger mortgage through benefit of tax relief or option mortgage subsidy

Tax relief is a great help to people buying houses on mortgage. You will appreciate the advantages even more if you know that not long ago you would have to pay *extra* tax for the privilege of owning a house. That somewhat unreasonable and illogical levy, Schedule A tax as it was called, has been abolished, and nowadays the arrangement runs entirely the other way: when you start buying a house on mortgage you begin to pay *less* tax.

How this comes about is explained in detail below. The details are interesting but apart from their intrinsic interest it may be well worth your while to master them, even if it takes a bit of effort, because tax relief is the basis for some advantageous special mortgage arrangements which may be of direct benefit to you (*see Chapter 6*). However, for the moment let us dwell on the main immediate point that the direct practical effect of income tax relief (or option mortgage subsidy) is to reduce a houseowner's monthly outgoings: and it is on this basis that the mortgage seeker is put in a position to negotiate a bigger mortgage. Or to put it another way: Tax relief or subsidy will leave more money in your pocket: therefore you are able to afford to take on a bigger mortgage commitment.

Let us see now how the system operates. Tax relief is achieved through a Government dispensation that the amount of interest paid on a mortgage shall be deducted from the housebuyer's income before tax is charged. The easiest way to grasp how this works is to picture in your mind the four parties involved in the arrangement. The one in the middle is you. The second, sitting in his branch office, is the building society manager. The third is the inspector of taxes, sitting in *his* office. The fourth is your employer.

The building society manager grants you a mortgage and you undertake to repay the debt in agreed instalments month by month. You also agree to pay an extra sum, to be included in the regular monthly payments, to give the building society a return on its operations, and this extra sum, of course, is the interest.

You begin repaying the mortgage and the next thing you know is that your employer seems to have given you a rise. There is more money in your pay packet or your salary cheque is bigger.

It's almost as though you are being rewarded with a regular monthly bonus for having taken out a mortgage. And indeed that is the effect. However, the reward comes not from your boss—although he is the channel through which you receive it—but from the other shadowy figure in the affair, the inspector of taxes.

He has received from the building society manager a note, a mortgage certificate, reporting the amount of interest you are paying on the mortgage. The tax inspector credits this amount as an allowance on your tax file, gives you a new and more favourable PAYE coding, and sends this to your employer who thereupon makes up a bigger pay packet for you or writes a bigger salary cheque.

You will see from this that the bonus is real, direct and practically instantaneous on you beginning to repay a mortgage. Of course nobody is *giving* you anything—you are simply paying less tax. Nevertheless the phrase has been used 'Being paid to buy a house' and it is not so very wide of the mark; and tax relief on interest payments on a mortgage is one good reason for it still being better sense, to use a time-hallowed phrase, to 'rent the money to buy a house rather than pay rent for living in someone else's'; for there is no tax relief on rent.

You will have gathered that tax relief on interest on a mortgage is worth having. However, that is not the whole of it. You will also be given tax relief on any premiums (another word for 'payments') you expend on life insurance connected with your mortgage. Relief is not given on the full amount, only on 40 per cent, but it is a useful benefit all the same (*see Chapter 6, page 75 et seq*).

This extended explanation of how tax relief operates may seem artless to houseowners of long standing and seasoned experience. But first-time buyers do not always grasp the concept easily. Many indeed do not realise that it is there to be grasped. The Institute of Economic Affairs reported in 1968 that 58 per cent of houseowners interviewed in a study on housing said that they did not know about income tax relief when they first took their mortgages out.

However, there is no need for you to ponder deeply the mechanics of the tax relief arrangements. You should state on your annual income tax return the amount of interest paid to the building society for the year and give the number of your account at the society's branch office. But even if you neglect to do this the system operates and you get the benefit. If your mortgage is not with a building society but with a council or a friendly society, the arrangements are the same. However, if the mortgage is with another kind of lender—an insurance company, for example—you must ask the lender for a letter which you then send on to your tax inspector asking for a 'provisional allowance' of tax relief to be arranged: otherwise you must wait until the end of the financial year at the next March 31 to get the benefit. But although the system is not fully automatic in such a case the benefit is precisely the same.

An accountant studying the tax relief system would sum it up by saying that the effect of the benefit is to reduce the rate of interest on a mortgage from $8\frac{1}{2}$ to 6 per cent. He might also express it another way—that tax relief is worth 32p in the £ on the interest paid on a mortgage.

Deepish waters. Luckily all the calculations will be done by your tax inspector. But it does no harm to have a glimmering of the basis on which he works.

Now, let us agree that the tax relief system is very useful indeed if you are earning a lot of money and paying a lot of tax but not nearly so good if you are not very well off, or have more children, and do not pay very much tax or pay no tax at all. This unfairness was the subject of comment and criticism for some time and at last something was done about it. That 'something' was the introduction of the option mortgage subsidy scheme in 1968, and now benefit similar in effect to income tax relief is enjoyed by housebuyers who pay little or no income tax and who before the new scheme was brought in had to pay the full real cost of their mortgage interest while better-off people paid less.

Why is the new scheme described as 'option'? Because you can opt for it as an alternative to tax relief: the choice is yours. Once having chosen, you are committed for four years—you cannot change back. You cannot ask for the subsidy benefit at the beginning of a mortgage and then very soon afterwards, as your income rises or your children cease to be dependants, say you would

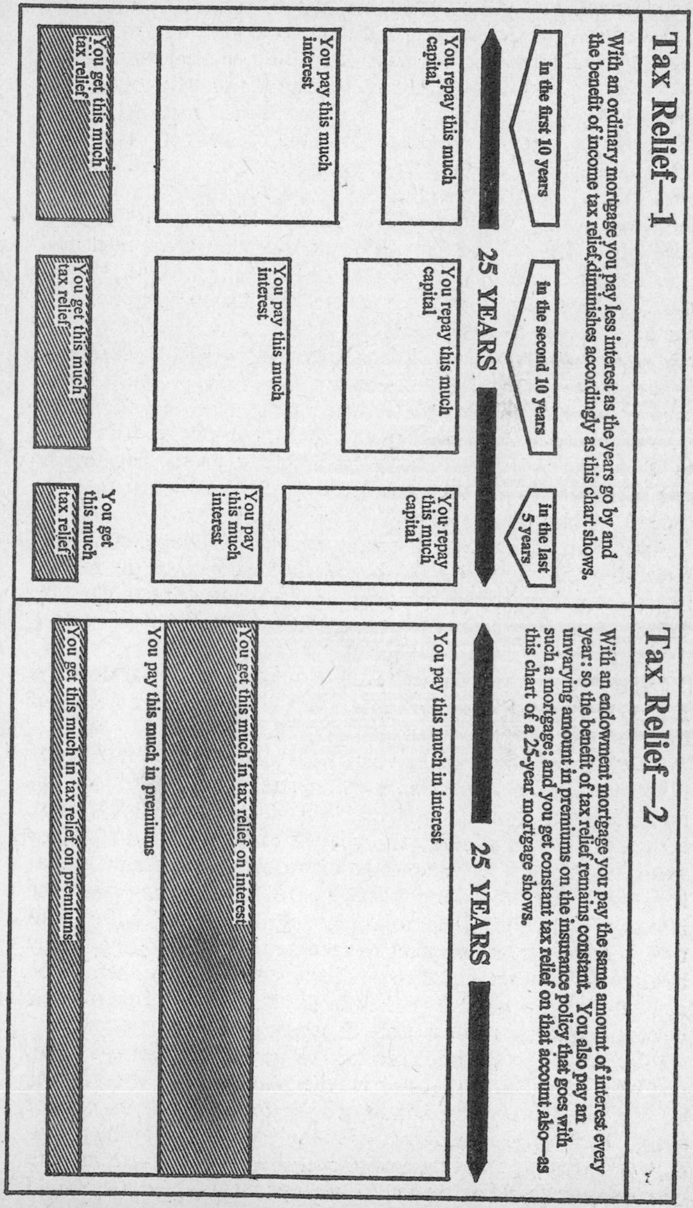

Tax Relief—1
With an ordinary mortgage you pay less interest as the years go by and the benefit of income tax relief diminishes accordingly as this chart shows.
25 YEARS
in the first 10 years
in the second 10 years
in the last 5 years
You repay this much capital
You pay this much interest
You get this much tax relief
You repay this much capital
You pay this much interest
You get this much tax relief
You repay this much capital
You pay this much interest
You get this much tax relief
Tax Relief—2
With an endowment mortgage you pay the same amount of interest every year: so the benefit of tax relief remains constant. You also pay an unvarying amount in premiums on the insurance policy that goes with such a mortgage: and you get constant tax relief on that account also—as this chart of a 25-year mortgage shows.
25 YEARS
You pay this much in interest
You get this much in tax relief on interest
You pay this much in premiums
You get this much in tax relief on premiums

prefer to claim tax relief instead. However, there is nothing to stop you ending the mortgage before four years and taking out another one, switching from subsidy to income tax relief as you do so. It would be a drastic step, though, unless you were changing houses anyway, because apart from anything else you would probably have to pay a redemption charge* penalty for redeeming the mortgage early.

What benefit does a housebuyer get from the subsidy? Not quite as much as the standard rate taxpayer gets from tax relief. The subsidy (which is paid by the State) will reduce the housebuyer's interest rate by about 2 per cent, unless the full rate is 6 per cent in which case the subsidy will be given at a rate to reduce the rate to 4 per cent, not lower. Another exception: On an endowment mortgage (see Chapter 6, page 75) the subsidy will be 1¾ per cent and given only on the mortgage interest, not on the insurance premiums, on which you will continue to claim such tax relief as you may be eligible for.

There is a helpful rule to guide you to a decision whether to take the subsidy or claim tax relief. If you are paying less than 30s a week in tax the subsidy is very probably the best arrangement for you. Note that you can if you wish opt to go off tax relief and on to the subsidy if you think it worth your while.

Most building societies and insurance companies and all councils operate the option mortgage subsidy scheme. Members of housing associations or housing societies can benefit from tax relief or block benefit of the subsidy: and this has been one main reason for the rapid development of the 'coownership' form of housing societies in recent years (see Chapter 11).

You can get a bigger mortgage through the 100 per cent mortgages scheme

The scheme was introduced in April 1968 to enable people of modest means to buy on no deposit terms or with only a small deposit. It was made possible by a special arrangement between the Government and the building societies.

You can ask for a 100 per cent mortgage from a building society or local council but you should not apply unless you are genuinely hard pressed. The scheme was devised to help people whose efforts to amass a deposit cannot contend with rising prices, or not so well off people who don't earn enough to save.

Old or new houses can be bought under the scheme. But

---

* See Glossary.

valuation (*see Chapter 1, page 14*) may fall short of the asking price—especially with older houses—in which case the mortgage will not be a 'no deposit' one because you will have to pay in cash the difference between price and valuation.

Of course you will also have to have some cash in hand, even if no deposit is called for, to pay the usual fees and charges (*see Chapter 2*), including a premium on the mortgage indemnity arrangement which is the basis of the scheme.

A house bought under the scheme must cost no more than £7500. More expensive houses do not qualify. Building societies will apply their usual income rules, that the mortgage loan should not exceed about two and a half times annual gross income or that monthly income should not exeed weekly outgoings. The scheme is linked with the option mortgage scheme, meaning that you must accept the subsidy, not tax relief.

You may wonder how the building societies were persuaded to relax their traditional insistence on a deposit. The answer is really our old friend mortgage indemnity. The basis of the scheme is that the State gives a guarantee to the building society jointly with an insurance company, thus covering the element of 'risk' normally covered by the buyer's deposit. The State makes no charge to the borrower—indeed by taking over a fraction of the insurance company's proportion of the risk it achieves a slight reduction in expense.

You can get a bigger mortgage through a housing group
Strictly speaking, housing group ownership is not housebuying at all (*see Chapter 11*). However it is a modern and interesting means of housegetting, having some of the advantages of ownership and none of the disadvantages of renting; and it is financed in such a way that the terms to the members are in effect low-deposit 40-year mortgages.

You can get a bigger mortgage if you are a sitting tenant
If you are renting a house and are a tenant protected under rent legislation the value of the house, to the owner and on the open market, is rather lower than it would be if it were empty and could be sold with vacant possession. Therefore if the owner should offer you the chance to buy you can expect a building society to give you a higher percentage mortgage, perhaps 100 per cent, because the 'risk' element is low or negligible by usual standards.

Here is a story, of the Golds. They had been tenants for 20 years in a house in London SW18. They and another tenant were paying rents controlled at 1957 levels and at length the owner of the house decided the game was no longer worth the candle and gave the Golds, who had been model tenants, 'first refusal' to buy the place.

They jumped at the chance of becoming owners of the whole of the house half of which had been their home as tenants. The owner's asking price was £1750 and in addition, as was to be proved, about £1500 needed to be spent on renewals, redecoration and repairs. The Golds raised a mortgage from Wandsworth council repayable over 15 years at a fixed rate of 6 per cent, and the deal went through.

Subsequently they paid the remaining tenant £350 to leave and so became effective outright possessors. The house, a four-storey Victorian villa, has a real value now of £8000, and by letting the upper half furnished to four Australian girls at £10 a week the Golds underwrite their mortgage repayments. It is a case that well illustrates why sitting tenants may be rated high for a mortgage if the chance is given them to buy—although, of course, no one should rely on subsequent sub-letting to underwrite their costs in this kind of mortgage situation or any other. The Golds were lucky, but most people find that mortgagees (i.e. lenders of house purchase money) debar sub-letting, to furnished or unfurnished tenants.

You may get a bigger mortgage on an old house through claiming council grants

New high grants for the modernising of old houses are explained in detail in *Chapter 9*, but in brief grants are available up to a maximum of £1000 for the improvement of an old house. On such a house unfortunately a building society mortgage will generally be smaller than usual; but if the idea of modernisation attracts you you may reasonably quote the new high grants as in effect augmenting your deposit.

You can get a second mortgage to make up purchase price

But you would not be well advised to do so. As we noted in *Chapter 4* second mortgages are second class propositions for any housebuyer and certainly for anyone taking out a mortgage for the first time. The trouble is that even if you have been warned off the system you may not recognise a second mortgage when it is offered to you under another name, like 'loan to make up the deposit'. So it is a good idea to make yourself acquainted with the principle and you will know such offers for what they are.

Note first of all that second mortgages do not come from

building societies. The building societies offer *first* mortgages and that's that. These first mortgages, as we have seen, are usually low, about 80 per cent as a rule, because that is as much risk as the building society is prepared to accept and also possibly as much as it is prepared to lend you on the strength of your income and prospects.

You may think your mortgage rating should be higher and you may also think that the building society's idea of 'risk' is unduly cautious, but that is not a good reason for taking on the burden of a second mortgage offered from some other source. Such a mortgage is called 'second' because it comes second to a first mortgage and the risk to the lender is a second class risk—which means a big risk—and he will charge you high accordingly. The repayment period will be short, nothing like the 20 years or 25 years of a building society first mortgage: the interest rate will be high: and interest will be charged on the whole sum through the whole period. In a word, it will be highly profitable to the lender and highly expensive for you.

Luckily a building society will generally debar a second mortgage being arranged as a means of making up the difference between the first mortgage and the price of a house. But some societies may not and then the temptation becomes real and the housebuyers may succumb, ignoring or not realising the fact that a second mortgage is a heavy extra cost and a burden throughout the early years of occupation of a house.

You may raise a second mortgage after you have been in your house for some while, when your repayments on the first mortgage plus the increase in the value of your house will have built up 'equity' as security for further borrowing. This is somewhat better financial sense than taking on a second mortgage to help push through purchase in the first place, and you can put such a 'householder's loan' to good use—improving the house (in which case you can claim tax relief on the interest), buying a car, having a holiday. It still remains an expensive way of borrowing, however, and you will be better off with a 'further advance' from your building society if you can get it.

Such a mortgage is called 'second' because it comes second to a first mortgage and the risk to the lender is a second class risk—which means a big risk—and he will charge you high accordingly. The repayment period will be short, nothing like the 20 years or 25 years of a building society first mortgage: the interest rate will be high: and interest will be charged on the whole sum through the whole period. In a word, it will be highly profitable to the lender and highly expensive for you.

Luckily a building society will generally debar a second mortgage being arranged as a means of making up the difference between the first mortgage and the price of a house. But some societies may not and then the temptation becomes real and the housebuyer may succumb, ignoring or not realising the fact that a second mortgage is a heavy extra cost and a burden throughout the early years of occupation of a house.

You may raise a second mortgage after you have been in your house for some while, when your repayments on the first mortgage plus the increase in the value of your house will have built up 'equity' as security for further borrowing. This is somewhat better financial sense than taking on a second mortgage to help push through purchase in the first place, and you can put such a 'householder's loan' to good use—improving the house (in which case you can claim tax relief on the interest), buying a car, having a holiday. It still remains an expensive way of borrowing, however, and you will be better off with a 'further advance' from your building society if you can get it.

CHAPTER SIX

WHICH MORTGAGE IS BEST FOR YOU?

BUILDING SOCIETIES OFFER a number of mortgage schemes. Among them may be one that is especially helpful for you.

We have seen in *Chapter 4* that there are a number of sources for mortgages, and we have seen in *Chapter 5* that there are ways in which you may be able to get a bigger mortgage than at first sight you seem entitled to.

Now let us see what *kind* of mortgage you may have. To some extent this inquiry is similar in its aim to *Chapter 5*—to discover how you may get a bigger mortgage or lower repayments. But it will also cover mortgage arrangements suitable for people who can afford to pay *more* than usual and are prepared to do so for the sake of long-term advantage.

The mortgage most people have is an annuity mortgage

Also known as a decreasing mortgage or repayment mortgage. Really the best name for it is 'normal mortgage' because it is the most straightforward kind and the one that most people have when they buy a house for the first time.

It is best for most people because it is the simplest. In asking for such a mortgage you will naturally try to get as big a loan as possible but there is really not a great deal you can do except put into the balance all the income that you think and hope is eligible for consideration—overtime, commission, part-time earnings, wife's earnings and so on. If you are fortunate a building society will be tolerant: you have probably noted in *Chapter 4* the names of two building societies who will take a useful proportion of wife's income into account and apart from these two you may come across others similarly or more accommodating: it is the kind of lead you will be on the lookout for.

An annuity mortgage arrangement is the simplest of all because you simply borrow the money and undertake to make regular equal payments until the mortgage has been paid off at the end of 20 years or 25 years of whatever the period is. However, something that some people find hard to grasp is that although the monthly instalments never vary, the capital debt to the building society is paid off only slowly at the beginning of the mortgage but very fast towards the end. The capital debt, of course, is what you owe to the building society for the lump sum loan it has given you to buy the house: the other part of your 'debt' is the interest on the loan: and just as your overall debt thus falls into two parts so the building society will regard your monthly instalments as being in two parts, the first of which is credited as reducing your capital debt and the second of which is credited as reducing the interest you are committed to pay.

Let's take a practical example, using figures. Let's say you borrow £3500 on mortgage repayable over 25 years at 8½ per cent. Your monthly instalments will be £28·50. Every year then you pay a total of £342: and at the end of the 25 years you will have paid a total of about £8500. What a lot of money to pay back considering that you only borrowed £3500 in the first place! It's £5000 more than you borrowed—and that £5000 of course is the interest.

We might imagine that at the building society office there will be two files with your name and number of mortgage marked on them. One file is headed *Interest 'debt' of £5000* and the other is headed *Capital debt of £3500*. In the early years most of the £28·50 you pay every month is marked up in the first file as reducing the interest and only a little of it is credited in the second file as reducing your capital debt. Gradually however as the interest is reduced an increasing proportion of the £28·50 is marked up in the second file as reducing the capital debt: until in the last years of the 25-year mortgage term there is practically no interest outstanding and the last of the capital debt is being wiped out at a fast rate (*see diagram on page 63*).

On the face of it none of this is really of much practical import to you. After all, as far as you are concerned the only things that matter are, first, that on a £3500 annuity mortgage— to take our example—you will pay a regular £28·50 every month; and, second, that eventually the whole debt of £8500 will be paid off. However, there is one slightly disadvantageous effect for you in an annuity mortgage—that with such a mortgage you will get a lot of tax relief in the first years, rather less and in decreasing amounts in the middle years, and practically none towards the end. And we can say this is slightly unfortunate because it is in the middle years of a mortgage that your general financial burdens will be greatest—with children at school, family holidays, running a car and so on—and it is a pity there-fore that while your bills during this period will continue to include an unvarying cheque every month to the building society your 'tax rebate' will get smaller year by year.

However, things may not actually work out this way in practice. Most people change houses about every seven or eight years and in selling your first home and buying another you may decide to take out another kind of mortgage altogether under

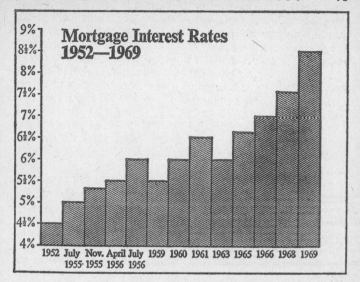

which interest is repaid at a constant rate and tax relief is therefore unvarying (see later).

What happens if interest rates* change after your mortgage begins? Mortgage interest rates have changed 13 times since 1952 (*see diagram*) and very likely there will be some changes in the future. There have been six changes since 1960, only one of them a downward one, and so it might be reasonably hoped that the next variation will be down. If the change is a downward one you have nothing to worry about—your monthly repayments will be reduced. If the rate goes up, however, your monthly repayments could be increased. You may be offered the choice of paying a higher sum every month or having the mortgage period extended: but if the increase is a big one or if there is a succession of increases there will come a point where your monthly repayments fail to reduce the outstanding interest obligation, meaning that the mortgage becomes a perpetual one, and the building society will insist then that you make bigger monthly payments.

To sum up: An annuity mortgage is the simplest and most common arrangement. You should try to have as much of your income and wife's income taken into account as you can to get as big a loan as possible, but otherwise the mortgage offers no

---

* *See Glossary.*

scope for special negotiation. You will pay a fixed sum every month but in the early years of the mortgage tax relief will be high, in the middle years middling and in the late years low. If interest rates go up either you will pay more each month or the mortgage period will be extended.

A useful variant is the joint income mortgage

This is an annuity mortgage in which both the husband's and the wife's incomes are taken into account so enabling them to borrow a larger amount. It is designed for people newly married or about to be married, and the mortgage is taken out in the joint names of the couple.

A joint income mortgage is based on the assumption that for the first three years of marriage the wife will continue to work and will be able to contribute towards the mortgage repayments: but after three years, the reasoning goes, the couple will probably have a baby, the wife will cease work, and the family will have only one income, the husband's.

Accordingly the mortgage is so arranged that in the first three years the monthly repayments are high but after that are reduced. How high will the instalments be at first? So high that if they were maintained at that level the mortgage would be cleared in 15 years! Obviously at such a rate of repayment a useful amount of debt is wiped out in the first three years, but what happens after that? The mortgage is rearranged. How? By the remaining debt being spread over a 25-year repayment period. The result: the instalments are reduced to a level which can easily be met from the husband's income alone.

Of course a couple may not start a family in three years—there is nothing in the mortgage agreement to make it obligatory—and their joint incomes may continue, enabling them to keep up a high level of repayments to clear the mortgage in 15 years. But although such a high rate of repayment may cheerfully be borne for three years or so it could become a burden if maintained for much longer, and so the building society may agree to rearrange the mortgage over 25 years anyway.

The main advantage of the scheme is obvious—a couple can get a bigger loan on the strength of their joint incomes even though the first mortgage period of 15 years is rather shorter than the customary 20 or 25. Another advantage, as we have noted, is that the high repayments in the first three years reduce the debt quite substantially so that if the couple decide to sell their house to buy another they will be able to carry a larger sum forward for the new purchase. A disadvantage of the system is that a higher interest rate* may be charged.

Another useful scheme is the variable term mortgage

This is an annuity mortgage taken out over a longer period than usual, say 30 years, with the result that repayments are low, or alternatively that a bigger loan is forthcoming for a given income. The arrangement is described as 'variable' because the borrower has the option at any time of increasing the size of his monthly repayments.

The scheme is designed for young salaried staff—in other words, securely placed people whose incomes can be expected to rise steadily as the years go by. This factor of well-based salary expectations is one that is often taken into account in favour of borrowers, by the way, whether or not the variable term system is proposed.

An escalator mortgage gives you a 35-year loan

Again this is an annuity mortgage. But it is offered initially on a 35-year repayment term. The first year's repayments are based on the 35-year term, but in the second, third, fourth and fifth years the repayments are stepped up (hence 'escalator') so that the final effect is that the mortgage is repaid in about 24 years.

You will guess that, again, expectations of rising income are taken into account with such a mortgage, and indeed it is designed for the borrower who is on a salary scale which will increase by known amounts, or a known percentage, every year. A figure reckoned as the basis for the arrangement is a rise of 3 per cent a year, and if the salary increase is rather more than that the monthly repayments rule (weekly income must equal monthly repayments—*Chapter 5, page 56*) is relaxed slightly to *first years' total repayments must not exceed 25 per cent of annual income*, which is a more favourable basis for the borrower.

For the few—'interest only' mortgages

Also known as standing mortgages and fixed mortgages. The system is not of much use to most people but you will find it helpful to understand how it works because the basic principle can be adapted to produce two other mortgage schemes ('half repayment' scheme and endowment mortgage—see later) which are practicable for a number of people.

'Interest only' means what it says. You repay only the interest and none of the capital debt. Two questions at once come to

---

* *See Glossary.*

mind. The first is: How then is the capital debt ultimately repaid? and the second is: Surely the total interest on such a mortgage amounts to a very large figure?

To take the first question: Yes, this is the snag. The building society will want the capital debt repaid at some time—of course—and as the monthly instalments are geared to repay only the interest, the capital debt will eventually have to be repaid in a lump sum. That is why the scheme is of use to only a few people— those who can look forward to an inheritance or some other certain gratuity in future years.

The answer to the second question again is: Yes, the total interest does amount to a very large sum. You can see why. Not a penny of the monthly repayments is devoted to reducing the capital debt and consequently the interest stands at an unvarying high level. If you borrow £3500 over 25 years at 8½ per cent on 'interest only' terms you will pay about £25 a month: which is about £300 a year: making a total repayment of £7245 over the 25 years. And after all that you have to repay the capital debt of £3500!

Of course, let us not forget the magical influence of tax relief. If the interest stands at a constant high level throughout the 25 years then tax relief will remain a constant benefit, not dimishing as the years go by—as happens, you remember, with an annuity mortgage (*see diagram on page 63*). Herein lies the attraction of the 'interest only' principle when it is adapted to the other schemes we will be discussing in a moment.

One last word on 'interest only' mortgages. The biggest mortgage you can get under this arrangement is 66 per cent. So you can see its usefulness is indeed limited.

'Half repayment' mortgages may suit some borrowers
Unfortunately 'half repayment' mortgages also are limited to 66 per cent, which reduces their attractiveness. Again they are based on the borrower's expectation of some money coming to him in future times to clear the capital debt. That said, it can be noted that the system is more practicable than the 'interest only' scheme because only half the loan is taken on an 'interest only' basis: the other half is repaid as a straightforward annuity mortgage.

This may puzzle you slightly, but it needn't. Here is an example with figures. You want to borrow £3500 and you choose the 'half repayment' method. The loan is split into two parts of £1750. On one part you repay the interest only: on the other part you repay part interest, part capital debt. Over 25 years at 8½ per cent the 'interest only' payments amount to about £12.40 a month:

which is about £149 a year: a total of £3725 over 25 years. The interest-and-capital repayments are £14 5s a month: and the total interest over the 25 years amounts to about £2500.

Let's not forget tax relief. You will get constant tax relief benefit on the 'interest only' half of the mortgage and diminishing benefit on the annuity half.

A pause for reflection

By now you will have grasped one or two key facts about the various kinds of mortgage scheme. If you are still not quite clear, go back to the beginning of this section and start reading again. Don't worry if you have to do that: not many people do understand mortgages very clearly, and some don't really get the hang of the system until they've been repaying one for a few years.

Let us restate the basics. You borrow money to buy a house. The size of the loan depends primarily on your ability to repay. There are ways by which your income can be, so to speak, stretched—that is, made to go further.

Income can be stretched by overtime, wife's earnings and so on being taken into account. It can be stretched by benefit of income tax relief or option mortgage subsidy being taken into account (*see Chapter 5, page 60*). It can be stretched by the mortgage being arranged over a longer term than usual. Finally it can be stretched by repayment of the capital debt being partially or wholly deferred so that you need repay only the interest month by month.

It is the last stratagem we have been investigating in the last couple of pages. We have seen how the basic principle is an 'interest only' mortgage and how this can be modified to yield a 'half repayment' mortgage method. Now we shall examine a mortgage scheme which meets in an adroit way the problem of how the deferred capital debt can be repaid.

An endowment mortgage is a good scheme if you can afford it

'If you can afford it . . .' To them that hath shall be given yet more—a cynical phrase, but sadly an accurate one and as true of mortgages as of anything else. If you are not very well off you must make do with an ordinary kind of mortgage and feel glad that you got it. But if you are somewhat better placed and your earnings enable you to pay interest on an 'interest only' mortgage *and* make payments on a life assurance policy as well you may end up rather better off than the other chap.

The new thing, you will note, is the life assurance policy. We have not mentioned life assurance so far but with endowment mortgages it begins to play its part. As it happens, later in this section you will be able to read some advice about taking out insurance to 'protect' your mortgage in case you die before it is paid off; and you will learn that such protection insurance is generally independent of the mortgage agreement. In the case of an endowment mortgage, however, the protection is integral and automatic, a built-in part of the arrangement. It is not the main part, though, useful as it is. The main part is a promise given to the building society by the insurance company that the company will repay the capital debt in a lump sum at the end of the mortgage term. This promise is given in return for you agreeing to take out an endowment assurance policy with the company. The policy will run as long as the mortgage—20 years, 25 years, 30 years, whatever the period may be—and you will pay a fixed amount every month, the premium on the policy, to the company throughout the term.

Thus you take on two liabilities—monthly payment to the building society of the interest on the mortgage: and monthly payment of premium to the insurance company. You will see now why this scheme is not for people of low or average income.

For those who can afford it it is a neat scheme because the premiums to the insurance company also rate for income tax relief: not the whole—only 40 per cent—but useful nevertheless. The result is that over the term of the mortgage the total cost is about the same as for an annuity mortgage *plus* the cost of separate mortgage protection.

There is something else yet. We said earlier that with an endowment mortgage you can end up rather better financially. How is this achieved? Simply, you ask for an endowment policy which yields a cash bonus at the end of the mortgage term. Such a policy is described as a 'with profits' policy, and that means exactly what it says—the insurance company sets aside part of the profits of its business for you. You will be notified at intervals of how the profits are mounting up and at the end of the term you will receive the accumulated profits to date in a lump sum of some hundreds or thousands of pounds, as well as having your capital debt to the building society paid off.

Of course, you will pay higher monthly premiums on a 'with profits' policy. But again you get income tax relief on a proportion of the extra amount you pay, so the real cost is reduced.

However, pondering the profits that would come to you under such an arrangement, you may shrewdly observe that sums of hundreds and even thousands of pounds will have a much less impressive real value in 25 years time or so when the mortgage period is complete and you collect. Against that is the fact that you will be garnering the fruits eventually of the insurance

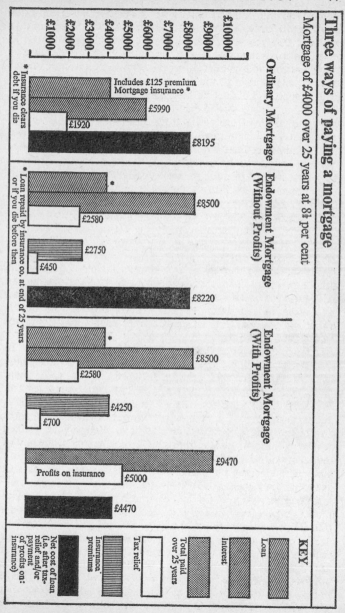

Three ways of paying a mortgage

Mortgage of £4000 over 25 years at 8¼ per cent

£10000 £9000 £8000 £7000 £6000 £5000 £4000 £3000 £2000 £1000

Ordinary Mortgage

Includes £125 premium Mortgage insurance *
£5990
£1920
£8195

* Insurance clears debt if you die

Endowment Mortgage (Without Profits)

*
£8500
£2580
£2750
£450
£8220

* Loan repaid by insurance co. at end of 25 years or if you die before then

Endowment Mortgage (With Profits)

*
£8500
£2580
£4250
£700
Profits on insurance £9470
£5000
£4470

KEY

Loan

Interest

Total paid over 25 years

Tax relief

Insurance premiums

Net cost of loan (i.e. after tax relief and/or payment of profits on: insurance) company's business activities in the intervening years, and if you have been able to choose a company with a good proven record on profits you will have hedged nicely against inflation. And of course the real value of your monthly payment falls as the years go by.

Another point. We have discussed 'annuity mortgages' earlier and we are discussing 'endowment mortgages' now as though the two systems were like oil and water, never to mix. But the mortgage set-up as the whole of this section is intended to show you, is a very much more flexible one than many people realise and you may be able to get a 'part annuity, part endowment' mortgage if you ask for one. Why should you want to do this? One good reason may be that you already have an endowment policy which would cover part of the loan, and you could use this policy to get an 'interest only' loan for its value and borrow the remainder of your house purchase money on an annuity mortgage. Apart from that, you may be able to arrange a 'part annuity, part endowment' mortgage if you are attracted to the benefits of the endowment mortgage system but cannot afford the outgoings on a thoroughgoing endowment mortgage arrangement.

If you want to link your fortunes more directly with expansion and profit in coming times you can arrange an *equity-linked* policy under which the major part of the premiums you pay will be invested in shares.

You would be wise to consult a good insurance broker if you are interested in this kind of mortgage arrangement—a member of the Corporation of Insurance Brokers or the Association of Insurance Brokers (*see Chapter 4, page 52*). Make sure that you do not take on anything more than you can afford, and bear these points in mind: 1 The insurance company should have a good record on profits if you are to get real value from a 'with profits' policy; 2 The building society may charge a higher rate of interest on a mortgage linked with an endowment policy; 3 If you can, you should choose a 'with profits' policy under which you collect profits just *after* a periodic announcement of profits by the insurance company.

A lot of words, but not by any means too many for an exposition of this interesting and valuable mortgage method. Words are necessary, of course, but in the end it all comes down to figures, and here are some which show how a 'with profits' arrangement scores over others.

We assume that the mortgage is for £4000 at $8\frac{1}{2}$ per cent. If you borrow this sum on an annuity mortgage and 'protect' the mortgage with an independent insurance arrangement, the total cost of having borrowed to buy the house over 25 years will be £8195.

If you take out an endowment mortgage, without profits but automatically incorporating mortgage protection, the total cost of having borrowed to buy the house over 25 years will be £8220.

If you take out an endowment 'with profits' mortgage, which of course incorporates automatic mortgage protection, the total cost of having borrowed to buy the house over 25 years will be £1170.

The chart on *page 77*, makes these comparisons absolutely clear.

You can note that an endowment mortgage can be arranged in association with option mortgage subsidy (*see Chapter 5, page* 60). Instead of tax relief on the interest paid the interest rate is reduced by 1¾ per cent: and you claim such tax relief as you are eligible for on 40 per cent of the premiums on the policy.

What happens if interest rates* rise after you take out an endowment mortgage? Unfortunately you will not be able to have the period of the mortgage extended for the simple reason that the term is related to that of the insurance policy, which is unalterable. So you would have to increase your monthly repayments. If interest rates *fall* you will pay less each month—of course.

To sum up then: An endowment mortgage is an 'interest only' mortgage linked with a life assurance policy. Your total monthly payments are higher but because the level of interest remains constant you receive undiminishing income tax relief. You also receive constant tax relief on part of the payments on the insurance arrangement. Protection of the mortgage is automatic. Disadvantages are that a higher interest rate may be charged on the mortgage, and if interest rates go up then monthly mortgage repayments must be increased.

A variety of ingenious schemes

Some enterprising building societies seem to take pleasure—and a good thing too—in devising new schemes based on a life assurance link. One, by the City & Metropolitan, results in periodic reduction of interest rates* on account of the insurance premiums being invested directly with the society. How this is done cannot be explained in a few words, but it does not really matter. The interesting thing about the scheme is that by signing up for the life assurance an intending housebuyer may put him-

---

* *See Glossary.*

self in line for a no-deposit mortgage two years later. It sounds worthwhile, and doubtless is: a consultation with an insurance broker (*Chapter 4, page 62*) would show how it compares with other arrangements.

Whatever kind of mortgage you have you should protect it

This is only good sense. In taking out a mortgage you are assuming a large debt. You trust and hope that you will be able to maintain the monthly repayments but it may turn out that through some hazard you are unable to. You may die before the debt is paid off: or you may become incapacitated and no longer able to work: or fall ill for a short while and be short of money: or suddenly have to meet some urgent expense that prevents you from keeping the monthly repayments up to date.

Many people fear this happening, an emergency forcing them to interrupt their repayment of a mortgage, and worry themselves to death over it. Of course it is not pleasant to find that you cannot meet your commitments in life for some unhappy reason beyond your control, but there is really no reason to dread it. If something does go wrong the sensible thing is to tell the building society straight away. Go along and talk to the branch manager about it preferably. He will very likely suggest that you cease payments for a while with the society's consent, or pay only interest for a time, or have the mortgage rearranged to bring about a reduction in payments. His concern will be as keen as yours that you get safely through the difficult period, and he will be as resolute in trying to avoid the worst coming to the worst and the house having to be sold for the society to get its money back.

If it does come to that extreme point, the society will ask a court to give a possession order and will sell as soon as it can. It will be obliged to get the best price possible, and after taking the money due to it must hand the remainder to you. If your mortage is a council one the council is obliged to sell by auction and if you are not satisfied with the sum that comes to you you can take the matter to arbitration.

As we have said already, it is wise to take out insurance to cover the risk of you dying before the mortgage debt is clear, and it is worth taking the extra small step of arranging for the insurance to cover the monthly repayments if you fall ill or have an accident which interrupts your earnings. Such an arrangement is made through a mortgage protection policy, and almost certainly when you take the mortgage the building society will offer to arrange it for you with an insurance company with whom it has an association.

CHAPTER SEVEN

FREEHOLD OR LEASEHOLD?

WHEN YOU BUY A FREEHOLD HOUSE you become the absolute owner of the house and the land it stands on.

A leasehold house, in contrast, stands on land which continues to belong to someone else.

That 'someone else' is the landlord. You are the lessee or the leaseholder. The land is occupied by you, in your house, on lease. One day the lease will run out and the landlord may take his land back, and with it the house. Meanwhile you will pay him a 'ground rent'—say £8 a year or £12 or £15—in acknowledgment of the fact that he is the owner.

Obviously it is much better to buy a freehold house than a leasehold one. But sometimes the term of a lease will be so long that buying the house is practically the same as buying freehold—999 years for example. But a much more usual period is 99 years.

If the house is an old one not much of the lease will be left, assuming it was for 99 years to begin with. You wouldn't feel very confident about 'owning' a house where the lease had only 10, 15 or 30 years to run. Nor would a building society feel very confident about giving you a mortgage to buy it. On the other hand you would feel quite happy about buying a brand-new house on a new estate where a 99-year lease is only just beginning to run, and a building society would normally grant a mortgage readily.

Raising a mortgage for a leasehold property

The crucial thing in leasehold buying, indeed, is whether you can raise a mortgage on the property. With houses, most lenders will baulk at a lease which has less than 50 years to run or where there will be less than 25 years life left in the lease at the end of the mortgage term. The same consideration applies to flats. It is in any case harder to get a mortgage for a flat or maisonette (*see Chapter 8*) although paradoxically it is still generally true that building societies prefer to lend on leasehold flats and maisonettes rather than on freehold ones. The reason for this is that through mutual agreements and covenants* attached to the leases of all the flats or maisonettes it can be ensured that the block as a whole will be kept in good order and of pleasant appearance, and the building society's interest is thus protected.

* See Glossary.

Local councils are generally more tolerant in giving mortgages on leasehold houses and flats (and flats and maisonettes generally) than building societies (*see Chapter 4*). They will be less insistent than the building societies that the remaing life of the lease be substantial. However, it is probably wisest to ignore short-life, leasehold propositions altogether. If house ownership is your aim go for a long-life lease or leave leasehold alone. All the same you may care to note that leasehold ownership has been put in a new light by the Leasehold Reform Act of 1967 and short-lease opportunities may occur of which profitable advantage can be taken. We will look at this later in this section.

Covenants and apportionments

A lease will almost certainly have covenants* attached to it committing you as to what you may or may not do in and around the house, or flat. Naturally you will study such covenants carefully and seek a waiver of any that you feel you cannot accept, or drop the deal altogether.

There is a second point you should take note of as a leasehold buyer. You remember from *Chapter 2* that the completion of the process of buying a house involves apportionments—small sums due to be paid by you to the seller. In the case of leasehold buying these will very likely include the items of ground rent and fire insurance paid in advance and beyond completion* date by him.

The lease, by the way, may name an insurance company a lessee *must* use in which case the existing policy must be endorsed with your name when the responsibility for insurance passes to you at the time of exchange of contracts* (*see Chapter 2, page 24*). If your building society says that it wants its own preferred company to be the insurer the point would have to be argued out.

Leasehold bargains?

Let's briefly look at the Leasehold Reform Act and its effects. The Act enables a leaseholder to buy the freehold of a house (not a flat) from the landlord, or have the lease extended 50 years at increased ground rent. The price for the freehold will be the value of the site plus the value of a higher ground rent over 50 years, the value of the house being ignored. The value of the site is to be calculated as if the leaseholder were the only person in the world interested in buying it—in other words, something like 'sitting tenant' terms which as we have seen in *Chapter 5, page 66* are highly favourable.

---

* *See Glossary.*

The leaseholder qualifies for this right after having lived in the house for at least five years. Obviously some leaseholders in occupation when the Act came into force were in for a windfall—those who had taken on their leases towards the end of the term. Equally obviously the value of short-life leases has gone up since the Act came into effect, because at the least the leaseholder can get an extension of 50 years: and at best, a good best, can get the freehold on favourable terms. You may think that because the market will have adjusted itself in this way there are no more bargains to be got, but that is not necessarily so.

Two hypothetical cases

To see why, let's invent a person, Mrs Goulding, widow, the leaseholder of No 31 Long Street, Dulwich, south-east London. Mrs Goulding has just followed her husband into the hereafter, bequeathing the house to her son Anthony. He has a house of his own and so his only interest in No 31 is to dispose of it as quickly and as profitably as he can. The lease has only 13 years to run and on that basis the house is not very attractive to buyers. Mrs Goulding for some reason hadn't taken advantage of the new Act to buy the freehold or have the lease extended by 50 years, and Anthony cannot do so because he hasn't occupied the place as leaseholder for the requisite minimum five years. All he has to offer then is a 13-year lease and although in fixing his price he will try to weight it high in view of the benefit a new leaseholder will get under the Act after being in occupation five years, clearly he is not in a strong bargaining position. So it is that an alert househunter may get No 31 as a snip.

Let's suggest another case. Let us resurrect Mrs Goulding, reinstate her as leaseholder of No 31, but change her situation. Instead of living in the house she has for some years been sub-letting it to a tenant, Mr Burlington. Mr Burlington dies and Mrs Goulding decides to sell the place. But the lease is near the end of its life, and so again the house must go on the market hopefully weighted in price in view of the benefits available to a buyer under the new Act but with Mrs Goulding in no very strong position to stick out against any confident and know-ledgeable negotiator.

Bargains may be had, then, but it would be wrong to pretend that the chance of one like this coming up is more than marginal. The main point to grasp is that the 1967 Act has had the effect of making leasehold properties no longer the inevitably declining assets that they were: and a good thing too.

CHAPTER EIGHT

FLATS AND MAISONETTES

WHAT IS THE DIFFERENCE between buying a house and buying a flat or maisonette?

With a house you have the advantage of owning a distinct property standing on your ground, surrounded by your garden and reached through your own front gate. You have privacy and a strong sense of individual ownership and independence.

Owning a flat or maisonette is different. Above, below and to the sides of you are other owners separated from you only by floors, ceilings and walls. The gardens outside—or on the roof— are used by you and your neighbours in common; the path to the ground-floor entrance is a walkway for you all; the stairs and lift are shared. Hanging out the washing, keeping pets, painting your door a distinctive colour, may not be allowed.

Clearly it is preferable to live in a house. *But* flats and maisonettes are cheaper because they are smaller, use less land, and have many common walls and a common roof. Because they are smaller, they are more convenient to live in and keep tidy and clean. Consequently they make good first homes for couples without children or with only one small child or two.

Bought on mortgage, they rise in value as year follows year, just as houses do, and when the owner comes to sell he can reckon on making a profit to carry forward to his next purchase, just as a houseowner can.

Raising a mortgage
It is harder to get a building society mortgage on a freehold flat or maisonette than on a leasehold one. But local councils are easier than building societies on this point and a council generally will give a mortgage when a building society will not (*see Chapter 4*).

It is easier to get a mortgage on a purpose-built flat than on a flat produced by conversion of an existing house. Again, councils are more helpful than building societies generally on this count: but some building societies are helpful all the same (*see Chapter 4*).

Responsibilities and restrictions
In becoming the owner of a flat or maisonette you will almost certainly have to accept responsibilities and restrictions which have reference to the comfort, convenience and rights of the other

owners in the block; and they on their part will have to accept similar obligations in reference to you. With leasehold places, these conditions will be written into the lease: with freehold flats they may be set out in a deed of mutual covenants.* Either way you will be bound by them.

Some of the conditions will be framed to ensure privacy, pleasure and peace for you all, and you will see the plain sense of them even though the effect for you personally may be irksome—as, for example, in preventing you from having a dog or hanging oddments of clothes out to dry in your balcony recess. Others may bind you to pay a proportion of the cost of a porter or caretaker for the block; the cost of a lift; the cost of cleaning hallway, staircases and passages, and of maintaining the gardens; the cost of hot water and central heating from a common boiler. You will also be bound to accept responsibility for the upkeep of some part of the building outside your own property or contribute towards the cost of it being done on behalf of you all.

Some conditions, more obscure and probably couched in lawyer's language, will be difficult for you to grasp at all, and you may well wonder just what their import is. The answer will prove to be that you and your fellow owners in your conjoined homes are promising each other rights—such as continued support for your walls from walls below and the walls below those, right down, to the foundations; and such as continued shelter by the roof; and such as being able to get in and out without hindrance or obstacle—things that as the owner of an individual house you would take utterly for granted but which in the much more complicated circumstances of a number of small homes all encompassed within one large roofed structure cannot, a lawyer would maintain, be taken for granted at all.

Such conditions of one kind or another attached to ownership of a flat or maisonette indicate why building societies, cautious lenders as they are in the best of circumstances, have never been too keen about giving mortgages on such properties: and especially why they are reluctant to lend on a flat or maisonette produced from conversion of an existing old house. If the main drain cracks deep down in the ground below you all—who puts it right? If a shared water pipe bursts—who pays the plumber? The obligation may be, indeed should be, made clear in the conditions attached to the transfer to each one of you of the ownership of his property; but as the building society sees it, the

* See Glossary.

responsibility becomes vague and diffuse when it stretches beyond you, the borrower of the society's money and the direct object of its interest, to some other persons or parties.

A practical and useful, and common arrangement, is the setting up of a management company to look after the block as a whole, all the owners being represented in the company or having a right to a say. If the properties are leasehold ones the common ground landlord can undertake such responsibilities direct, or through a managing agent, and this is one of the strong reasons why building societies favour leasehold flats and maisonettes.

Two final points
Never buy a flat or maisonette without having an independent survey carried out (*see Chapter 1, page 15, and Chapter 3, page 33*). Do not try to buy without benefit of a solicitor (*see Chapter 2*).

Note the difference between a flat and a maisonette. A flat is *on the flat*, that is its rooms are all on the same floor. A maisonette (*petite maison*—small house) is on two floors and has its own access door. A maisonette is probably better for private living, but a flat is cheaper as a rule.

CHAPTER NINE

MODERNISING AN OLD HOUSE

BUYING AN OLD HOUSE and putting it into shape is for some people a very satisfying way of making a home. It makes good money sense if the project is planned and carried out in a businesslike way because old rundown houses can be bought quite cheaply and a large part of the cost of improving will be met by the local council on a new scale of grants introduced by the Housing Act of 1969. When the work is finished the rehabilitated house should be worth much more than it cost to buy and put in order.

'Converting' and 'improving'—the difference

The Act which has brought in the new high grants makes a distinction between 'conversion' and 'improvement' of old houses and you ought to understand what the difference is. You probably would normally use the term 'conversion' in the popular sense of generally 'doing up' but the Act gives it a specific meaning—making extra self-contained dwelling units within an existing dwelling. Against that, the term 'improvement' in the meaning of the Act, is, well, simply improving a house as a one-family dwelling.

Thus if you buy a Victorian three-storey house with basement and turn it into a modernised home for yourself and at the same time convert the upper floor or basement or some other part of it into a self-contained flat, that is a 'conversion'. But if you buy the house and do it up as a single dwelling, that is 'improvement'.

Of course much the same kind of working scheme will be followed in both operations, as improvement takes place whether you are changing the interior of the house to provide more than one home or are keeping it as a one-family place. There will be things like rewiring, curing of rot, replacing of windows, re-roofing, installing a hot water system, eliminating damp, replacing old gutters, knocking down walls, providing central heating, laying new floors, modernising bathrooms, replacing old lavatory pans, replastering walls, boarding-in ceilings, and so on.

You may need planning permission

If in the course of improving a house you intend to refashion the interior drastically or add extensions to the building or similarly make some major alterations you will need planning permission, and you must avoid committing yourself to buy the house before

you are sure that outline planning permission* is forthcoming
or has been given. For minor work, planning permission* may
not be needed but approval under building regulations* may have
to be got.

Something else you must inquire about is whether any restrictive covenants* are in operation in respect of the house which
positively forbid conversion. Such covenants are not uncommon,
their purpose being to ensure that houses in a neighbourhood
remain as single dwellings, not changed to multi-occupation
and so detract from the quality of the area. These covenants are
not insuperable barriers to conversion: they can be discharged
or modified by order of the Lands Tribunal or by a county court.
But you should make sure the way is clear before you commit
yourself to buying the house.

You should also bear in mind that the general upgrading
of the house may result in an increase in rates.* Not inevitably,
but clearly the possibility should be borne in mind in making
an intelligent appraisal of the factors to be taken into account.

How much of the work can you do yourself?

A competent person can put down new floorboards, remove old
plaster and put up plasterboard, fit a small bore central heating
system, fit double-glazing, rehang doors, replace window sashes,
repoint brickwork, lay concrete, fit a new bath and lavatory suite,
put up a false ceiling, install a sink unit, build a fuel store,
fit new rainwater pipes, paint, and hang wallpaper.

You may try to treat woodworm and rot (*see Chapter 3,
page* 38) but no one would seriously advise it because an
imperfect job would be devastating in its effects. For this and
other work you will need to call in professionals—raising or
lowering floors, replacing or adding stairs, knocking down walls,
repairing or replacing drains, dampproofing, rewiring, fitting new
joists, replacing whole windows, rebuilding sections of walls,
reroofing, replastering, foundations work.

You may need a surveyor or architect

If your scheme involves changes in interior spaces, extension
of the building, new staircases, partitioning—in other words
drastic structural alteration—you should enage an architect or
chartered surveyor. A thorough professional survey before you
buy the house is essential (*see Chapter 3, page 33*) no matter
how you propose to get the work done subsequently: and if you

---

* *See Glossary.*

are intending to engage an architect or chartered surveyor and can get him in on consultations at this stage so much the better. There is a firm which specializes in undertaking all kinds of conversions: it is Countrycraft Homes, of Countrycraft House, Middleton Road, Banbury, Oxfordshire.

Finance is more readily available from councils . . .
Now for the money side of it. Local councils will grant mortgages more readily for the purchase of old houses than will building societies (*see Chapter 4*). It is not unusual for a council to advance 90 per cent but remember that the figure will be based on valuation (*Chapter 1, page 14*) which may be lower than cost. One council, the one at Brighton, buys up old houses in the town to sell again—lending the money under its mortgages scheme—to couples to improve with the help of grants; and with the principle of area rejuvenation enshrined in the new Act this kind of chance is well worth looking out for. It is a pity that the dry and official air of councils' pronouncements often masks the really interesting opportunities that town halls may be putting in people's way. So to bring the thing to life here is a case—from Brighton—of a young couple David and Josephine Pope. On the face of it they couldn't have been worse placed in the housegetting stakes. Josephine's wage was about £13 a week and David, two years her senior at 22, was still at college, getting about £12 a week from grants and part-time earnings. Even so, under the council's rehabilitation scheme for old houses they were able to become the owners of a tiny (two bedrooms, living room, kitchen) house in Newark Place for £1180. Improvements— converting one bedroom to bathroom, building a new interior wall, removing chimney breasts, curing damp, new plumbing, new wiring, new front and back doors—cost £800, of which the council provided £330 in grants. David had £100 saved up, sold his car for another £150 and got the remaining £1400 from his parents on a private loan to be repaid at £5 a week. In every way —size of family, size of costs, size of house—this is a miniature housegetting operation, but of course it suited the young Popes delightfully and in their circumstances represents a godsend– thanks to intelligent council deployment of grant funds. Many others might wish that such a chance would come their way, and it is bound to happen that like opportunities will begin to occur more commonly in other parts as the provisions of the 1969 Act come to be taken up generally. It is a sensible and simple thing to ask the town hall what is going on in the neighbourhood, or what plans may be in the offing.

. . . less readily available from building societies

Building societies will not normally lend more than 70 per cent of valuation on a house for modernising, perhaps rising to 75 per cent of a valuation based on total cost of purchase and modernisation. Some will not lend at all: the Lambeth, for example, refuses to consider giving mortgages on any pre-1919 house, unless exceptionally. On the other hand small local or specialist societies are more accommodating. The Property Owners Building Society will consider lending up to 90 per cent, with a 25-year repayment period, on houses built before 1919; and the Chelsea and South London will, if satisfied with the security (in the sense of value, not in the sense of being proof against burglars) of the house as it stands, lend up to 80 per cent.

You must have plans and specifications to show the building society what you propose to do at the time you make the approach for a loan. If you are thinking of converting a house to gain an extra flat for letting to a tenant you must be ready to be asked to pay a higher interest rate*: or receive an outright refusal from a building society who would otherwise have been helpful. If you are a professional active in property or housing or a skilled man whose job is directly related to housebuilding or the repair and maintenance of houses, you may find that you are considered more favourably for a loan as one who knows what he is about.

Building society caution over the modernising of old houses has two bases. The first is that your idea of what makes a charming improvement may not be everyone's. Indeed, the cleverer your scheme the more off-putting it may be to the average ordinary buyer who looms so large in building society ponderings, and the harder the house may be to sell in later times. The other concern is that however thorough a survey is, and however well thought out are your plans, some unknown serious fault may come to light after work has got under way, causing costs to shoot up.

Against this second reservation it can be argued, now that the 1969 Act is with us, that the risk is covered to an extent by a provision in the grants scheme enabling a council to increase its grant contribution to cover the cost of unforeseen works. As for the first point, it is only realistic to take account of the con-

---

* See Glossary.

servativeness of building societies and keep plans in restrained key if not actually dull.

On one count or another, financing the modernising of a house is not the easiest of operations. A building society even after having approved a loan may not advance the money until the work is completed, meaning that you will have to arrange a bridging loan* to buy the house and meet the cost of the work as it proceeds. If the money is advanced before completion of the work it will probably be paid over in two or three instalments at agreed points in the course of the job.

Again, however, the building society caution on this and other points may be relaxed as the effect of the new grants system becomes apparent. For example, the new high grants (up to £1000 for modernisation, up to £1200 for each unit produced by conversion) may come to be reckoned, and reasonably, as both testimony to the increasing acceptability of housegetting via modernisation and as a substantial cash guarantee underwriting the whole operation. It may even prove that a promised grant will be taken by a society as counting towards a buyer's deposit or as augmenting the deposit to a level where a higher mortgage loan may be made.

How the new grants system works

These are the rules. You must be the freeholder, or leaseholder with at least five years of the lease to run (short leases can make sense nowadays: see *Chapter 7*). After modernisation the house should have at least 30 years of useful life ahead of it.

You must send to the council with your application for a grant a builder's estimate, plans and specifications, and the official forms duly filled in. When approved, the grants may be paid by the council direct to the builder if you so wish. If you let part of the house eventually, the letting will be subject to rent regulation. If the work is not carried out in a certain time, say 12 months, you may have to repay the grant.

Grants are available under two categories ...

Standard grants

Let's say you have plans for a sound old house which is simply shabby and out of date. You intend to undertake no ambitious modernisation programme, but just give the place decent basic fittings. You would ask for a 'standard' grant of half the cost of the work, up to a maximum of £200, for the following:

A fixed bath or shower—maximum grant £30 or half the

---

* *See Glossary.*

cost of building a new bathroom attached to the house.

Providing a sink—maximum grant £15, and another £30 for bringing hot and cold water to the sink.

Providing hot and cold water to the bath—maximum grant £45.

Installing washhand basin—maximum grant £10 and another £20 for providing a hot and cold water supply to the fitting.

Installing lavatory—maximum grant £50, more if a cesspool or septic tank has to be provided.

Bringing in mains water—maximum grant half of cost.

You can have the jobs done one by one; and if some have already been done that will not prevent you from having grants for the other items. But if the jobs you propose to have done come to less than £100 in cost you may not claim a grant unless grant-aided work done in the previous three years brings the total cost above the £100 level.

Discretionary improvement grants

If you buy a house solely for your own occupation which needs thoroughgoing rehabilitation, including probably some or all of the improvements which qualify for standard grants, you can claim grants to meet half the cost up to a maximum grant of £1000. These larger grants are called 'discretionary improvement grants' and note the wide meaning of 'improvement': it implies more than giving the house just basic decent fittings: it means having the place turned into a good dwelling by work of a high all-round level.

Indeed, the special usefulness of the new grants system is this: That grants may be claimed not only for straightforward improvement work but for a number of jobs, more or less expensive, which actually are repairs—such as dampproofing, roof mending, new drainpipes and gutters, rewiring, correcting defects due to settlement, renewing worn out or antiquated sanitary fittings; and making good damage unavoidably caused in the course of the work. Such repairs, including incidental costs, must come to no more than half the total grant: but their inclusion at all in the new system is a great advance.

If you intend to buy a house to convert it into two or more self-contained dwelling units, say flats, the maximum grant of

Modernising an old house—the new grants

Main part of house modernised and improved. Grant of up to £1200 covering work shown.

- New drainpipes and gutters
- Rebuilding part of wall to correct effects of settlement
- Removing interior wall to make enlarged room
- Mains water supply brought in.
- Rotted joists and floors replaced
- House rewired.

Basement converted into self-contained flat. Grant of up to £1200 covering of rot, rewiring, installation damp-proofing, treatment of lavatory and shower, sink, hot and cold water and structural work.

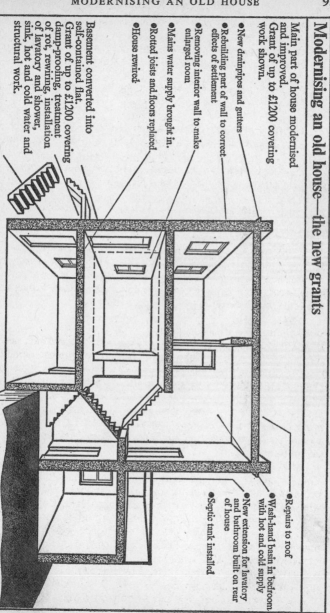

- Repairs to roof
- Wash-hand basin in bedroom, with hot and cold supply
- New extension for lavatory and bathroom built on rear of house
- Septic tank installed

£1000 may be claimed in respect of each unit. If the house has three storeys or more, basement counting as a storey, the maximum grant is increased to £1200 for each unit (*see diagram*).

As noted earlier, grants may be increased to help meet the cost of unexpected essential work disclosed after the work has begun. A word of warning: Councils need not operate the 'discretionary' part of the grants scheme, although all are urged to do so; and one council may differ from another in the way it applies the rules.

You can note that you may claim discretionary improvement grant up to a maximum of £1000 for knocking two or more houses into one, but you will have to satisfy the council that each of the original dwellings could not have been regarded as a satisfactory single home on its own or as capable of being made so.

100 per cent finance?

'Modernising an old house' means different things to different people. Well-off people envisage transforming a rambling Victorian villa into a gracious and spacious minor stately home. Impecunious couples think of the cheerful exercise of giving more light, new wallpaper, central heating, yellow doors and a reproduction coach lamp to a small terraced artisan's cottage from the turn of the century. Either scheme, or anything between, is practicable and may qualify for grants. However, a small enterprise—the artisan's cottage, say—fittingly enough may be in line for further assistance. If purchase and modernisation costs together come to less than £7500, or if purchase and modernisation costs, less grants, come to less than £7500, a 100 per cent mortgage may be sought under the State-supported scheme introduced in 1968 (*see Chapter 5, page 65*).

Alternatively, as noted earlier, an expected grant may be presented to a building society as an augmentation of deposit; or, under the 100 per cent mortgages scheme, as making up the difference between a loan offer based on a valuation below actual cost. The 100 per cent mortgage scheme is linked with the option mortgage subsidy, but since that too favours the not so well off the fact reinforces the tenor of the foregoing rather than weakens it.

CHAPTER TEN

HAVING A HOUSE BUILT
OR BUILDING ONE YOURSELF

HAVING A NEW HOUSE BUILT as your first home is quite feasible. However it is not necessarily cheaper than buying an existing house although you can cut costs by managing the job directly or by doing some or all of the building work yourself.

You will need to buy a plot of land.

You will need to raise a building mortgage.

Land is scarce and expensive in many parts of Britain. It is most expensive in or near cities, and in the south-east region of the country, but it gets cheaper away from conurbations and in areas of the north.

A house plot 30 feet by 26 feet in Devonshire Street in the West End of London was offered for £7500 leasehold in 1967, a value of about £420,000 an acre. Building land 14 miles out from London is presently costing about £48,000. At Southampton building land is about £26,000 an acre. At Wellingborough, Northants, it is £10,000 an acre, and in rural areas of the same county is about £5,000 an acre.

Sites for houses come in different shapes and sizes

For a semi-detached house you would need a plot with a frontage of at least 30 feet and a depth of 80 feet. A plot for a detached house should have a frontage of at least 40 feet and similar depth. For bungalows, plots with wider frontages are needed. Plots are sometimes sold with very narrow frontages for the building of three-storey 'town houses'. A plot may be part of an existing estate or built-up neighbourhood and have a frontage common to others, or it may be an individual site standing alone in an undeveloped area or an area where houses are few and scattered.

Here are two examples of how opportunities, sizes and prices vary:

Narrow plots with common frontages: At the time of writing nine housebuilding plots were being offered at the Isle of Dogs in east London at £6400 each. Each had a common frontage with the others. The frontage of each plot was 16 feet, the depth about 180 feet.

Normal shape plots with common frontages: At about the same time housebuilding plots were on offer by Scunthorpe council varying in size but typically of 30-foot and 40-foot frontages and

80-foot to 90-foot depths, with frontages common to other houses. Prices were from £625 to about £1200.

Ten ways to find land

You can write to estate agents (*see Chapter 1*).

You can study advertisements in newspapers (*see Chapter 1*).

You can look for a vacant plot between existing buildings or on a part-developed estate.

You can look for an abandoned or rundown house which can be demolished to make way for a new dwelling.

You can advertise in your local and regional newspapers or the journals mentioned in *Chapter 1*.

You can ask your council or county council if they have land to dispose of: or whether plots are available in an expanding area or redevelopment area where you would be prepared to move.

You can write to a New Town development corporation or the Commission for New Towns (*see Chapter 1*).

You can look for existing houses with long or big gardens. Big gardens are unfashionable and owners are often ready to sell part of an oversized area as a house plot with outline planning permission.*

You can consult a publication, *Survey*, a guide to individual building plots throughout the country, published at £2 by Barent Gold & Co of Duke Street House, 415–417 Oxford Street, London W1R 1BD.

You can write to builders. Some developers open up new estates partly or wholly to be disposed of in individual plots. One such in the north is William Whittingham's, a Wolverhampton-based firm. The arrangement is that the firm build the house for the client on the chosen plot: but in some cases the client commissions a builder of his own choosing to put up the house. Apart from such schemes, in times when operating finance is hard to get and builders are finding it difficult to get work you may be able to make a

---

* *See Glossary.*

similar arrangement with a small firm or master builder with land in hand which cannot otherwise be quickly exploited.

There must be outline planning permission for a house to be built

Town planning legislation requires that planning consent must be given before a house is built on a piece of land. The first part of this process is the granting of outline planning permission:* the second part is the granting of full planning permission* based on the detailed designs of the proposed house.

You must never commit yourself to buying a piece of land before outline planning permission has been granted. Sometimes you may feel an opportunity seems to good to miss as a speculative buy, but here is a story which will serve as a warning. An area of farmland at Horley, in Surrey, was divided into plots and offered for sale plot by plot during 1967 and 1968 on remarkably cheap and easy terms by a private company. The price per plot was about £490 and buyers were invited to pay in instalments. The company did make clear that outline planning permission for the building of houses had not been obtained, but intending buyers who inquired further, or had their solicitors make inquiries, found that the picture was rather different from what that simple statement might convey. The local planning authority was adamant that the land was protected by Green Belt policy and that permission for the building of houses on it would never be forthcoming. In other words, people who bought the plots gained nothing more substantial than a stake in a lottery which in the face of the unshakeable opposition of the planning authority would never yield a prize in the form of a completed house.

Outline planning permission can be applied for quite easily by the owner of the land or by you, acting with his knowledge and consent. Only a simple site plan need accompany the application. If you are anxious to secure an interest in a site for which outline planning permission is expected but not yet received you should pay a 'deposit to stakeholder' (*see Chapter 1, page 13*), making your offer subject to contract and conditional on outline permission being obtained. If something goes wrong and permission is not forthcoming you can withdraw without loss. Reputable developers offering plots on estates can be trusted to look after your interests fairly on this score, and it is hard to imagine any doubts about planning permission arising in such cases. How-

---

* See Glossary.

ever, one point to take note of: Where you are asked to make a deposit to secure your interest in a plot you should ask whether the deposit will be returned if for some reason the building of the house does not proceed.

What to look for in a building plot

It should be serviced—that is, have gas, water and electricity laid on. There should be main drainage, and if there is not your construction costs must include provision of a septic tank and a soakaway for rain water.

The site should be level for easy and economic building. It should be well drained and free from the risk of subsidence, with no culverts running underground. Land drains underground, although an aid to drainage of the soil, can impede trench digging and foundation work. The ground should not be made up—that is, reclaimed from former rubbish tips, from old mineral workings, from swamp—and the subsoil should be good for bearing a building—in order of quality, limestone, sandstone, chalk, clay.

There should be good and easy access, preferably over a made up road. Road charges* should have been paid or otherwise accounted for. You should ask whether any covenants* or restrictions will be attached to ownership of the land. In general the other considerations for choosing a site are those set out in *Chapter 1* relating to a desirable location for a house.

If the finished house is to cost £5500 or more you should arrange if possible to have the ownership of the land conveyed to you before building begins. The basis for this is that stamp duty* is charged on a rising scale in respect of houses costing £5500 or more. By having the land conveyed separately you keep the cost of the land out of the total price: if the house price is thus reduced to below £5500 you avoid paying any duty, or if it remains above £5500 you will pay less duty than if the cost of the land and the cost of the house has been taken into account as a total sum.

Finance for the building of a house

You must have capital in hand to buy the land or pay a substantial deposit to secure it. If you haven't enough capital you will almost certainly have to have recourse to a bridging loan,* because the usual lenders of house finance will not as a rule lend money for the purchase of land on the security of the land alone.

* *See Glossary.*

A lender, a building society say, wants to see a significant part of the building work completed before lending money under a building mortgage arrangement (see below).

Sometimes, however, when clients are having houses built on plots by a developer who is using this method as an alternative to offering ready-built houses for sale on an estate, the developer may ask for only a small or nominal sum as deposit and will bear the cost of construction himself until a stage is reached in the building of the house when a building society is prepared to let a building mortgage commence and advance money to finance the operation.

What is a building mortgage? It is a mortgage arrangement under which a building society, or other lender, agrees to pay fixed sums at certain stages of the building work. With this money you would pay the builder sums due to him in instalments under your agreement with him (the building contract: see later). He is then able to pay his merchants and his workmen and keep the job going. The lender pays over each fixed sum after receiving a report from his valuer on the work done to date.

Before agreeing to a building mortgage, a building society will want to see approved plans and a specification (see later). You will not get a building mortgage unless the house is to be built under the supervision of an architect, chartered surveyor or the National House-Builders Registration Council.* Interest on a building mortgage begins to run from the time of the first advance: payment of interest is usually deferred until the house is complete, at which point the total accumulated interest is deducted from the final advance. The full mortgage loan will be repayable over the usual extended term of 20, 25 or 30 years.

A building mortgage may well be of a higher percentage than is usual with housebuying mortgages, because the house will have a high real value in a building society's estimation. If your agreement with the builder has been a favourable one for you, or if you have done some or most of the work yourself (see later), so much reducing total cost, building society valuation may be *above* cost and in that case you could expect a 100 per cent mortgage. For these same reasons a mortgage may be offered on an uncommonly long repayment period—30 or 35 years.

Arrangements on building mortgages differ from building society to building society. Here are three examples: The Lambeth—25 per cent advance when walls of the house are up to first floor level, 30 per cent advance when the roof is tiled,

---

* *See Glossary.*

20 per cent advance when plastering is completed, 25 per cent advance on completion. The Civil Service Building Society—33 per cent when the roof is tiled, 33 per cent when plastering is completed, 33 per cent on completion of the house. The Woolwich—20 per cent at first-floor level, 15 per cent at roof plate level, 15 per cent at roof tiling, 25 per cent when plastering is completed, 25 per cent on completion of the house.

You can note that the last of these three examples, which have been chosen at random, is the most favourable because it provides for the greatest number of stage payments. The most helpful building mortgages are those which provide for the first advance of money to be made at an early stage of construction and for subsequent advances to be made at frequent intervals.

Your agreement with the builder

The agreement, the building contract, binds you to pay a certain price for the completed house and binds the builder on his side to meet certain definite obligations.

One of the most important conditions, price apart, is the completion date, and the agreement may incorporate a penalty clause under which the builder will indemnify you if completion is delayed beyond the agreed date.

The building contract will be related to a specification—a detailed statement of materials and fittings. It may also be related to a bill of quantities, a detailed breakdown with costs arranged by you. The contract would be a 'with quantities' one in such a case. Otherwise it would be 'without quantities', signifying that the builder will estimate those costs on his own account.

The building contract should state as exactly as possible the extent of the works that will be undertaken by the builder—that is, to state clearly whether the price is to include all fencing, gates, paths, provision of fuel store, clearing and levelling of garden, spreading of topsoil. It may be possible to have such works, or other jobs like decorating, *excluded* from the agreement with the object of bringing the price down, if you are willing to do the work yourself after moving in.

The building contract will set out the stages at which you will make payments to the builder. It is customary that 10 per cent be withheld at each stage, these retention sums to be paid after completion of the work when you are satisfied that all is as you wish with the house. The usual arrangement is that the stage payments be made to the builder after inspection of the completed work at each stage and the issuing of a certificate by the supervising architect, chartered surveyor or other agent.

If you are employing an architect or chartered surveyor to

supervise the building of the house the arranging of the building contract may be left in his hands. You can get a standard form of building contract from the Royal Institute of British Architects, 66 Portland Place, London W1.

A builder or developer may suggest that you reduce your non-building costs by sharing the services of his solicitor in the legal work involved in the arrangements. It may sound attractive but should not be accepted: the essence of legal work on property is that a solicitor should make searching inquiries to protect his client's interests and obviously this loses its real force if the same solicitor acts for both seller and buyer.

Finding a builder

You may secure a site for a new house from a developer under the arrangement already described whereby the developer will expect to build the house for you. Otherwise, if you are not proposing to build the house yourself (see later), you will need to find a builder. You can get names of builders in your area from the Federation of Master Builders, 33 John Street, London WC1; or the Federation of Registered House-Builders, 82 New Cavendish Street, London W1. A list of member firms is also published by the National House-Builders Registration Council,* 58 Portland Place, London W1.

Designing a house

A developer who sells you a plot linked with his building services will probably offer you a basic house design or choice of designs which you can have varied in minor ways. He will probably give you the chance of specifying extra fittings and features, or items of a higher standard than the basic specification provides for.

If you are buying a plot to have a house built independently you will have to design the house or have it designed for you. It is not advisable for an inexperienced person to try to design a house, and your choice is effectively either to pick an existing design suitable for the site and your needs or have a house designed for you.

You can buy books of house and bungalow plans and choose from the selection they offer. The following are typical: The *Daily Mail Book of House Plans*, the *Daily Mail Book of Bungalow Plans*, the *Planahome Book of Plans*, the *Homefinder Book of House and Bungalow Plans*, the *Arcplan Book of House and Bungalow Plans*, the *Ideal Home Book of House Plans*. There are

---

* *See Glossary.*

also the *Countrycraft Homes Book of Plans*, and the *Architectural Services Book of Timberframe Homes*, and *The Housing Enquiry Service Book of Home Designs*.

Engaging an architect

You can engage an architect or chartered surveyor to design a house for you. The Royal Institute of British Architects keeps an 'index of practices', with details of photographs of architects' work. It will also put you in touch with architects in your area.

An architect will survey the site before beginning to design a house. After discussions with you he will draw up a sketch design for you to consider. He will prepare working drawings, draw up a specification, and arrange with a quantity surveyor for a bill of quantities to be drawn up. He will apply for planning permission.* He will invite tenders—'tenders' are quotations—from builders. He will supervise the construction of the house.

Architects' fees are 10 per cent of total cost for work up to £2000, tapering to 6 per cent for work costing £16,000 or more. Thus in the middle range a fee would be 7½ per cent of the cost of a house between £4000 and £8000: the fee for a house costing £5000 would be £375. These are minimum charges, and higher fees may apply by agreement.

You may not want an architect to do anything other than design the house or design the house and obtain planning permission. For partial service a lower fee is charged.

The services of a chartered surveyor, and the terms, are similar. You can get the names of practitioners from the Incorporated Association of Architects and Surveyors, 29 Belgrave Square, London SW1; or the Royal Institution of Chartered Surveyors, 12 Great George Street, London SW1.

We have said that having a house built is not necessarily cheap

We have mentioned developers' schemes for building houses on selected plots. One has been quoted as an example of a high quality and very reliable offer, not as an example of a cheap way of getting a house built. The all-in price of a house built on a plot by Whittinghams ranges from £5875 in a rural locale to £11,140 in a good class city district. Obviously the factor of land values is crucial. However, there are ways of getting a house built at reduced cost, and we will look at these now.

---

* *See Glossary.*

Developer's profit can be eliminated

By buying a plot and independently commissioning a builder to put up the house you will save money. The all-in price will reflect the cost of the land, cost of materials and labour and builder's profit, but you will cut out developer's profit. Needless to say this takes a fair degree of confidence on your part, but of course it is not by any means uncommon. Much depends on the builder of course – and the architect, taking it that you do engage one. It would be unusual for an architect *not* to figure in such an enterprise – see the previous page.

You can reduce costs by managing the job yourself

If you think you have the time and the competence you can manage the job yourself. This reduces costs by giving you the benefit of discounts on materials and by eliminating both developer's profit and builder's profit.

Here is an example. Mr John Hellen, newly returned from district service in Africa, bought a riverside plot in Co Durham as the site for a house, and set about managing the job for himself.

He decided to simplify his task by ordering a system-built house which would be brought to the site in crates on lorries. The manufacturer's agents undertook to put the structure up (and also, incidentally, to obtain planning permission*). This left Mr Hellen to concentrate on the job of ordering materials and engaging workmen—to prepare the site, lay drains, put in the foundations and oversite base, glaze the windows, do the plumbing, raise chimney stacks and brick walling, and put the roof on.

He ordered materials from local merchants at trade discount rates and engaged his workmen by the hour or at agreed piece rates. For good measure he did some digging, concreting, painting and general labouring himself—unaccustomed work for him because he is a lecturer.

The result was a saving of about 30 per cent. The finished four-bedroom timber frame house had cost £7000, including £1000 paid for the land, and Mr Hellen estimated its value at about £10,500 on completion.

Cheapest of all is to manage and build yourself—either individually . . .

A person like Mr Hellen cuts out developer's profit, builder's

---

* *See Glossary.*

profit, gets benefit of trade terms, and further reduces cost by doing odd jobs himself. The ultimate is to manage the job yourself *and* do all the work, so cutting out all profit to other people except the vendor of the land and the merchants who supply you with materials, and any sub-contractors you may choose to employ for specialist or particularly difficult tasks.

Here is the story of the Webbings. Mrs Webbing had had a small windfall, a £1000 legacy, and the couple discussed the possibility of getting a house built. They were lucky in having the chance of a plot on an area just being opened up by the local authority at Wokingham in Surrey, and they went ahead.

The plot, about 45 feet by 90 feet, was large enough for a three-bedroom detached house with garage. The Webbings chose a design from one of the house plan books and Mr Webbing in conjunction with a friend who had taken the neighbouring plot went to work.

Brickwork, roof tiling and glazing were contracted out. Mrs Webbing and the friend's wife helped with the painting. The two men did most of the rest of the work between them, giving about 30 or 35 hours a week to the job.

After some 30 months of part-time work, the two houses were completed. The Webbings' had gas-fired central heating, cork floors to bedrooms, a downstairs lavatory and built-in wardrobes among its features.

Total cost was about £4250. The local authority had asked Mr Webbing to put down only 10 per cent of the purchase price of £1700 for the plot, leaving him with capital in hand to buy materials and pay his sub-contractors until advances from the building mortgage began to come in. The mortgage was offered by the local authority, repayable over 30 years at a fixed rate of $7\frac{1}{4}$ per cent. Today the house is worth £8000 to £8200 on its site 36 miles from London.

... or as a member of a group

You can build a house for yourself by combining with other people who have the same aim. It is as rewarding as other forms of independent building and it is easier because group activity is more efficient. However, you forfeit the advantage of individuality, because group-built houses of course stand together as a self-contained estate and they are usually alike outwardly although interiors may differ one from another.

Such groups normally operate as 'self build' housing associations (*see Chapter 11, page 117*) which gives them a useful corporate status for negotiating for land and raising finance. The basic procedure is the same for having a house built by other means—acquiring land, raising finance, engaging an architect, obtaining planning permission,* and proceeding with construction on the basis of stage payments under a building mortgage which enables merchants' bills to be paid month by month. Members of such groups are chosen for their special skills and management is usually vested in a small committee.

Finally—the element of luck

You ought not to rely on being lucky in any part of the house-getting process—but you ought not to discount the chance of good fortune altogether.

Here, to close this section, is the story, from Cumbernauld in Scotland, of the lucky Mackays.

With their four children, the Mackays were living in a rented house. They heard that options were being offered on building plots in another part of the town and that the offer, by the local development corporation, was not only of plots but of design and construction as well.

The Mackays inquired and found that they were not required to contribute towards costs but only sign a letter confirming their interest. The architects produced an outline design which they then discussed with the Mackays to ascertain and incorporate their wishes. Building went ahead and after about a year the house was complete.

It had four bedrooms, the main bedroom having its own bathroom. There was also a family bathroom, a cloakroom downstairs, a playroom for the children, central heating and double glazing.

The cost was £5760, plus £580 for a garage: not exceptionally cheap perhaps, but far from dear. And the Mackays were offered a 100 per cent mortgage at a fixed rate of 6¾ per cent.

It seems almost too lucky a break to be true, but the fact is that the local people were anxious to make a success of a new small area of private houses and so offered this exceptionally attractive package deal—land, design, special features, construction, plus a 100 per cent mortgage. Just chance, you might say: but the point does not need underlining that chances can crop up anywhere at any time. And the Mackays' experience is a happy story to close a section on how, with or without the special blessing of fortune, you can in one way or another set about getting a brand new house built for yourself.

---

* See Glossary.

CHAPTER ELEVEN

HOUSING GROUPS—GETTING A HOME TOGETHER

A HOUSING GROUP IS A NUMBER OF PEOPLE who combine together to provide homes for themselves on easier terms then they can get as individuals.

Housing groups are to housegetting what packaged tours are to holidays: the end product for the client is much the same but he gets it cheaper, more conveniently and without having to be involved in the details (see *How to join a housing group, page 118, this chapter*.)

Housing groups have their natural home in Scandinavia, where most people get their homes in this way. In Switzerland one house in seven is provided by groups: in America the system made its mark in New York in the fifties when a six-year spurt produced 20,000 new homes.

In Britain, housing groups have been coming on steadily since the early part of the 1960s, but they are not yet very widely known about or understood.

Groups provide homes for their members in many ways

By buying existing houses, flats or maisonettes.

By having new homes built.

By the group building new homes itself, all the members sharing in the work.

By buying up a big old house to improve and convert. When large grounds come with the house a group may also build new homes on the land.

In short, housing groups can do any of the things an individual may do—buy existing houses, build new ones, modernise old ones. They can also do something an individual would not normally do, which is buy, build and convert in combination.

However, there are disadvantages to be taken into account. So let us look at the whole picture.

Housebuying is normally a complicated business . . .

To appreciate a strong advantage of the housing group system, its convenience, let us compare it with the conventional individual housegetting procedure. Let's review, briefly, the complex business of finding and buying a house in the ordinary way.

Finding the right house in the right neighbourhood is an operation on its own (*Chapter 1*). We have to engage a professional surveyor to inspect it and assure us that it is in good order (*Chapter 3*): and if it is not we must negotiate a reduction in price, or find extra money for repairs, or call the whole thing off and start all over again. We have to ask for a building society valuation which may prove to be below price (*Chapter 1*), obliging us to find ways of augmenting our resources. We find ourselves having to pay a number of charges—valuation fee, surveyor's fee and so on.

Throughout we have to act rather more carefully and legalistically than is natural to us: we have to apply caution to the handing over of a preliminary deposit (*Chapter 1*), we have to remember not to commit ourselves too early to a binding agreement to buy (*Chapter 1*). If we are thinking of buying at auction we must learn and remember the special rules which can have the effect of trapping us into an unwanted and undesirable purchase (*Chapter 1*).

We have to deal with a solicitor and trust him to look after our interests in a transaction most of which is incomprehensible to us. We have to try to be intelligent over details of minor transactions coincidental with the major one of transfer of ownership, like agreements over fixtures and fittings and apportionments (*Chapter 2*). We have to know what 'freehold' and 'leasehold' mean (*Chapter 7*), what covenants are, and so on.

To buy the house we have to have enough cash in hand to meet all the side costs (*Chapter 2*) and then enough to make up the difference between the building society's mortgage offer and the price (*Chapter 2*). We have to understand how tax relief works, or the option mortgage subsidy (*Chapter 5*). We have to explore ways of getting a bigger mortgage if we can (*Chapter 5*), and examine different kinds of mortgage scheme to see whether one or other is particularly favourable for us (*Chapter 6*). We have to arrange protection of the mortgage in case we die or fall ill and cannot keep up the repayments (*Chapter 6*).

If we want to build a house we must add to all these obligations the search for land, the negotiating of planning permission, and the arranging of special finance (*Chapter 10*). If we buy an old house to modernise we must commission a surveyor, an architect, a builder; we must find the money; and we must apply for grants (*Chapter 9*).

... it is much simpler done through a housing group

In striking contrast, as a member of a housing group you need do no more than enrol, take out a share, put down a deposit, contribute your ideas on design, and then sit back and wait for your house, flat or maisonette to come up. Legal matters, surveys, valuations, mortgage raising, are dealt with on your behalf by a nucleus, a committee, advised by specialists or perhaps having specialists among its number. Of course, you may be in the nucleus yourself, since the arrangement is basically a democratic one, but you need not be if you don't want to be.

The housing group system is cheaper

Instead of the individual members of a group having to seek separate mortgages a group negotiates a block mortgage to buy houses, build new ones or modernise old ones. Such block mortgages can be arranged over 60-year, 40-year, 35-year and 30-year terms: consequently monthly repayments by the members once they are in their homes are lower than is usual with individual mortgages which, as we know, are normally for 20 or 25 years.

Further, block mortgages raised by housing groups are often 100 per cent or 90 per cent. A group which intends to build new houses can secure 100 per cent finance to cover purchase of land plus cost of construction; in contrast to what we noted in *Chapter 10* that an individual who wants to have a house built must have capital in hand, or be able to raise a bridging loan* to acquire the land—because building societies will not lend for purchase of land nor let a building mortgage begin to run until a significant part of the building work has been completed.

Because a group may get a high percentage mortgage its members need contribute only low deposits to secure their homes—sometimes as little as £50 or £100. Further, members do not have to meet bills for legal work (apart from a fee for a lease), valuation, survey and other charges, including architect's fees, because these costs are included in the overall financing arrangements and are largely covered by the high percentage mortgage.

The fact that monthly repayments after occupation are lower than on an individual mortgage is of special benefit to middle-aged or elderly people who in the normal way would have to commit themselves to high repayments on a short-term mortgage of, say, five to 15 years. Tax relief can be claimed by members on their monthly repayments, or the group may collectively claim benefit of option mortgage subsidy to bring about a reduction in monthly payments for all. Repayments are inclusive—covering

---

* *See Glossary*

rates, insurance, outside maintenance, possibly garden maintenance, and management costs. They might also cover heating
and hot water from a central system, porterage (at flats), the cost
of a lift, and the cost of communal arrangements like laundry
centre, nursery, playroom or meeting room.

Another advantage is ease of selling

A group may require only that a period of notice be given by a
departing member. Often a waiting list system ensures that a
newcomer is available to take up the lease if the departing
member cannot or does not find a buyer himself.

However, there are drawbacks

You can never own your home.* Your housing group home
belongs to the group always. You occupy it on a lease, completely
secure in tenure but never an owner—except in the sense that
you have an equal share in ownership of all the group's properties
('coownership').

You get only partial profit on resale. If you live in the house
for a minimum period—three or five years—you will, on leaving,
get a proportion of the increased value but not the whole of it.
The proportion may be 30 per cent, 50 per cent, 80 per cent or
some other level, but whatever it is it will have been stated in the
original agreement between you and the group. It follows, of
course, that one of the things you will ask before joining a group
is how much of the profit you will get if you leave. If it is only 25
or 30 per cent you may hesitate: if it is 50 per cent or higher you
may be well satisfied in view of the favourable low-deposit and
repayment terms.

Whether or not you live in the house the minimum period
before leaving you will get back your original deposit, your
nominal share of about £5, and any part of your monthly payments which has actually helped the group reduce its capital debt
on the block mortgage.

You have to get involved with other people to greater or less
extent as a member of a housing group, and if you are a person
who prefers to remain uninvolved this will seem a drawback to
you.

You may get a house you don't very much like, and that must
count as a disadvantage of the system. However, it is not a strong
possibility. As a member of a small housing group you would
expect to have a say in the siting, design, layout and fitting-out

---

* *Unless the group is a 'self-build' or 'independent' one*—see later.

of the house which is to be yours. If you join a large group which has already planned, designed and possibly finished its homes, you may well be given the choice of one of a number of houses, flats or maisonettes.

Housing groups can be cumbersome and slow in carrying out their plans, and this is a real disadvantage. A certain kind of group known as a *coownership housing society* (see later) has to go through a complicated procedure to acquire land and raise money, and this results in delay. However the process can be speeded up if the group enlists the help of one of a number of big permanent societies which have come on the scene in recent years (see later).

Other groups known as *housing associations* (see later) are perhaps less prone to procedural delays. All the same, in raising finance from local authorities they may be held up while committees and officials deliberate, and they may also experience checks, with consequent delay, over their use of council grants for modernisation.

A particular kind of group, the '*self-build*' *housing association* (see later), in which the members actually build homes for themselves, is obviously a long-term enterprise. Four years from start to finish is not uncommon, and the period may be longer.

Independent groups (see later) are less liable to delay. But like all kinds of group they must take time for consultation and debate among their members.

Summing up the pros and cons

The disadvantages of the group system are not to be discounted and a homeseeker would have to weigh up the pros and cons and decide for himself if this relatively new development in the British housing scene is for him. The simplicity of house-getting through groups is strongly in their favour: so is their financing capability: and clearly their steady progress in recent years has been due to their offering a new kind of solution on these two main counts to the problems that individuals encounter in seeking to buy a home for the first time. To recap, they offer homes on low-deposit, extended mortgage terms, with complete security of tenure, freedom from concern over details of purchase and maintenance, benefit of tax relief or subsidy, and prospect of capital profit on moving away, with quick resale sometimes virtually guaranteed by a waiting list system. Against that, mutuality can have its disadvantages, and the system can be slow: a member doesn't get all the profit on resale, and he can never enjoy full and outright ownership—except, as noted, with 'self build' and 'independent' groups.

Coownership houses near Edinburgh.

Coownership maisonettes in Worcestershire.

How groups differ in their structure

As we will see, both public money and building society money is being steadily deployed for housing groups, and often either existing houses or areas of land are put in the way of groups or offered on special terms when an individual would get no such favoured treatment. Parliamentary legislation has been framed to include provision for groups, and public authorities generally are well disposed towards them.

You may guess from this that groups operate under some kind of set of rules which have the approval of the Government and councils, and up to a point you would be right. However, there is nothing to stop people establishing groups which operate as private limited companies or in an entirely informal way if they wish.

Let us see how different kinds of group attain their aims: and let us study some examples of how the group system has been used in different ways by different people in different parts of the country.

'Independent' groups—for better-off people

Emphasis has been placed on the cheapness of getting a house through a group. This does not mean, however, that all groups operate at what you might call economy level: some are set up by quite well-off people attracted by the advantages of group action but not unduly concerned about arranging easy term finance.

Let's imagine that a few such people join together to have houses built for them. Jointly they take an option on a piece of land. They have the houses built, raising the finance in one of the usual ways, split the costs between them, move in and live happily ever after: end of story.

Such a group is an 'independent' one. It would bind itself to no set of rules apart from what the members may agree among themselves. It would raise its main finance where it could, not rating, or wanting to rate, for any special financial treatment. It would use building societies, banks for bridging loans,* and would probably require its members to contribute directly from their capital, or raise private loans to meet a substantial proportion of costs. Obviously this is the kind of operation suitable for people who have good financial resources and what you might call 'nous'. Not all of us have both or either, but for interest's sake let's look at two such group schemes from real life and see how they achieved their aims, noting that both were high-cost operations.

Seven people formed a group to buy a large old house and grounds at Blackheath in south-east London. Their object was to have the house demolished and on the cleared site have seven houses put up, one for each of them.

They decided to operate as a private limited company. Initially each member raised a bank loan or independent mortgage for about £2000 to help pay for the purchase of the site. Construction, by a contractor, was financed by a building mortgage arranged with the Halifax. The outcome was seven architect-

---

* *See Glossary.*

designed houses produced at an all-in cost which perhaps was 15 or 20 per cent less than their market value. This useful margin of saving was mainly the result of cutting out developer's profit, and was obviously one good reason for these seven people setting up their own company to buy land and get their houses built. They had an advantage, it may be noted, in being able to count an architect, builder and solicitor among their number.

Here is another story of an 'independent' group operation.

Again, seven people were involved. Again, a London site was chosen. Again the seven formed a limited company to acquire the land and have the houses built upon it.

The site was marked into seven plots and it was arranged that each of the seven members as a nominee of the company would buy one of the plots from the vendor, providing the money out of his own capital or by raising a private loan. Cost of the building of the houses was to be met under a building mortgage arrangement. When the houses were finished, the company would be wound up and each of the seven settle in, owner of his own home, paying off the cost on an independent long-term mortgage.

Costs: Each plot cost just over £4000, to which construction costs of about £12,200 were to be added. The estimated value of the completed houses was about £20,000 each. So again there would be considerable benefit from elimination of developer's profit.

Housing associations—for the well off or not so well off

Let's take a different kind of case now. Let's assume that a number of people, at least eight, set up a housing group to buy a site and have new houses built on it for themselves. Not all of them may have a great deal of money or able to raise any substantial private loan. Such a group must somehow get finance on favourable terms if it is to carry out its plans.

Its first step is to form itself into a *housing association*, registering as such with the Registrar of Friendly Societies, 17 Great Audley Street, London W1. It then affiliates to the National Federation of Housing Societies (NFHS), 86 Strand, London, WC2. As a housing association it will agree to adopt certain rules drawn up by the NFHS; and it will be able to negotiate for land and finance with a special status.

Each member takes out a £5 share and buys association Loan Stock to the value of the contribution—the 'deposit', if you like— required from him. This gives the association funds in hand for management expenses and a margin for working capital.

This capital, however, will be well short of what is needed for the purchase of land and the construction of houses. The association *might* go to a building society for a building mortgage, but it would not expect to get a loan to cover the purchase of the land (*see Chapter 10*), nor would it get any longer-term mortgage arrangement than an individual. Consequently the association would look for finance to its local council, which can receive it favourably as a registered association operating under recognised rules.

The council may make land available to the group if it has not yet found a site for its houses, and it will also be empowered under Section 119 of the Housing Act of 1957 to lend the money for purchase of the land and construction of the houses. Such a loan may be 100 per cent and be offered over a 60-year term. It should be noted that if the money is borrowed under a different enactment, Section 43 of the Housing (Financial Provisions) Act of 1958, the loan being repayable when the houses are completed, members can become outright owners of the completed dwellings by taking out individual mortgages which, lumped together, suffice to repay the council loan. In such a case the individual mortgages, raised from a building society or other customary source (*see Chapter 4*), could be expected to be more favourable than usual because valuation on the completed houses will be high, developer's profit having been eliminated from cost.

Housing societies—also for the well off or not so well off

Now let us consider a similar group of people who seek to acquire land and have houses built. But instead of forming themselves into a *housing association* they form themselves into a *housing society*. Why?

The reason is this. As a housing society the group will adopt the rules of the Housing Corporation, of Sloane Square House, London SW1. It will then be able to ask the Housing Corporation, in association with a building society, for 100 per cent finance to buy land and have houses built, the cost to be repayable over 40 years.

But this seems odd. Why set up a housing society to seek a 40-year loan through the Housing Corporation instead of setting up a housing association to seek a 60-year loan from a council?

One answer is that whereas a council *may* lend the money the Housing Corporation *will* (assuming the group is of serious intent and its plans are sound). The Housing Corporation is a special body set up to promote housing society schemes and it has been given funds specifically to finance schemes in association with the building societies.

Further, the Housing Corporation operates in conjunction with another body, the National Building Agency, which offers specialist services from which housing societies may benefit. Another factor is the existence, under Housing Corporation encouragement, of a number of big permanent housing societies whose role is to sponsor and develop new housing society schemes. A new group can attach itself to one of these 'big brothers' to its advantage: indeed it may decide to leave most of the work to the big society and be content to occupy and manage the houses when they are built.

Thus it is that nowadays housing groups are tending to set themselves up as housing societies—with the special title of "coownership' housing societies—rather than as housing associations, for the sake of benefiting from the Housing Corporation's special funding facilities and its associated specialist services. *

Is there then any useful main role left to housing associations who register with the NFHS? Answer—Yes, two such roles. One is conversion of existing houses, and the other is 'self build'; and we will be looking at both in a moment.

Meanwhile, let us complete this explanation of housing society operations by studying two successful schemes. One is in London. the other is in the West Country.

The London story centres on a block of flats, twenty all told, built as a five-storey building in the south-west of the city. The land was bought and the flats put up by a housing society called the Coownership Development Society, who raised their finance as a 100 per cent 40-year loan from the Housing Corporation and a building society. The group elected to receive option mortgage subsidy (*Chapter 5, page 60*) enabling a reduction to be made in the repayment terms for the members in the flats, which ranged in size from one bedroom to three bedrooms.

One member of the group is Mr Keith Whelan. On behalf of himself and his wife Janet he took out a £5 share and contributed a deposit of £300 to become the 'coowner' of a two-bedroom flat on which his monthly repayments are about £29 inclusive. If the Whelans move away they get back their £5 share, their £300 deposit and, if they have been in occupation for three years, a share of the increased value of the flat.

The other story is centred on an estate of 54 houses and

---

bungalows at Woodside, near Weston-super-Mare. The land was bought and the houses and bungalows put up by the Birkbeck housing society on 40-year 100 per cent finance raised from the Housing Corporation and a building society. Again this housing society elected for benefit of option mortgage subsidy to reduce members' monthly repayments.

One of the members is Mr Michael Pengelly. He enrolled for a £5 share and put down a deposit of £100 to make himself 'coowner' of a two-bedroom bungalow on which his monthly payments are £24 inclusive. If the Pengellys—they are a young couple, not long married—move away the £5 share and £300 deposit are returned, together with a share of the increase in value, assuming they have lived in the bungalow for three years. It can be noted that, with developer's profit having been eliminated from first costs, it is estimated that values of the Birkbeck homes would rise sharply by about 45 per cent in the first three years; and a coowner moving away after that time could expect to receive about £300 as his share of the profit.

'Conversion' housing associations
We have said that the housing association formula retains much point when purchase and conversion of existing houses is intended. A 'conversion' housing association can borrow money from a council over terms up to 30 years under Section 119 of the Housing Act of 1957, and it qualifies for benefit of option mortgage subsidy as an alternative to the claiming of tax relief, under Section 43 of the Finance Act of 1963. It can also claim council grants (*see Chapter 9*) for improvement and conversion work.

One possibility for such an association is the conversion of a large house into flats. Another is the purchase of a number of houses, perhaps in a row, for modernisation or for conversion into maisonettes, two to each house. A council loan can be negotiated to cover both purchase price and conversion costs, although as always valuation may be below real final cost in which case the contributions from the members must be of a size as to make up the balance.

Here is a case. The conversion of a Victorian house into three self-contained flats was undertaken by a housing association in one of the north-west districts of London. The house was bought and conversion costs met on a 30-year loan plus grants from Haringey council.

One of the members of the group is Mr Douglas Hill, a writer, who secured the top-floor flat in the converted house. The equivalent of the two-bedroom flat would cost about £5500 on the commercial market, and as a writer Mr Hill could not have expected a mortgage higher than about 65 or 70 per cent—meaning that to buy a similar flat privately he would have had to put down a deposit of about £1500. In striking contrast he got his housing association flat by taking out a £5 share and contributing £300, thereafter paying £32 a month, less tax relief, plus rates of about £4. If he leaves after three years occupation he gets back his share and deposit plus a proportion of the profit on the flat, the value of which is expected to rise by about 7 per cent a year.

'Self build' housing associations

A 'self build' housing association is in effect a mixture of housing association and 'independent' group. The basis of its operations is that it borrows money to buy land and building equipment and materials. Then, working in their spare time for two years or more, its members build the houses as a team. When all the houses are finished each member raises an individual mortgage on his allotted house, and hands the money to the group. With the total of these sums the group repays its outstanding debts, and winds up.

Such a group, registered as a housing association operating under NFHS rules, may seek a building mortgage from a building society, and it can be noted that the Co-operative Permanent looks especially favourably on such enterprises. However, the usual difficulty is that a building society is reluctant to lend money for the purchase of land on the security of the land alone, and accordingly a 'self build' association will customarily seek a 100 per cent loan from a council under Section 119 of the Housing Act of 1957 or Section 43 of the Act of 1958.

After the first advance to buy the land, the loan is usually made in instalments at agreed stages of the construction of the houses. The land itself may be made available by a council, with transfer of ownership—and therefore payment of purchase money—being deferred until all the houses are finished; or the land being transferred plot by plot as the work progresses. Interest is charged on the loan from the first advance, but usually payment of interest is deferred until the houses are finished. Group finances are augmented after a while by members paying 'rent' as they occupy the completed houses one by one.

Here is a 'self build' story. Mr Anthony Laker joined a 'self build' housing association at Haywards Heath, Sussex, as the plumber, which was his trade. He took out a share for a nominal sum and put in a further £30 as a contribution towards initial management expenses. His group obtained both land and finance from the local council.

After some two years of work the estate of a dozen bungalows was completed, Mr Laker and his eleven colleagues took out individual mortgages on their allotted homes, and the debt to the council was repaid. Mr Laker's three-bedroom bungalow cost £2800 and has a value today of rather more than £6000.

How to join a housing group

Study newspapers for announcements about new groups. Sometimes groups advertise for members in the personal columns.

Write to the National Federation of Housing Societies, 86 Strand, London WC2, for information about housing associations. Write to the Housing Corporation, Sloane Square House, London SW1, for information about housing societies.

How to form a housing group

Gather together by advertising or word of mouth a group of people of like mind.

Collect initial subscriptions to raise about £50 for preliminary management expenses.

Write to the NFHS or Housing Corporation as above.

CHAPTER TWELVE

GLOSSARY

Abstract of title   A précis of information which the seller of a house makes available to an intending buyer, through solicitors. It contains the essence of the proof of the seller's ownership of the house. It is made available to the intending buyer at the time of exchange of contracts (*explained in Chapter 2*).

Bridging loan   A loan, usually from a bank, to enable a buyer to bridge the gap between his present resources and his future expectations of mortgage finance. As far as the housegetter is concerned, a bridging loan would be useful for the purchase of land and the financing of construction in the building of a house; and in the purchase of an old house and financing of modernisation work.

Building regulations These are provisions governing building and development framed by and operated by local authorities. They cover matters like ventilation, air space, dampproofing, quality of materials, insulation and other factors relating to good habitation standards being maintained. Approval for work under building regulations and byelaws needs to be obtained even where planning permission may not be necessary. See also *Planning permission* below.

Completion   The meeting at which the representatives of the parties in a house transaction formally hand over to each other the documents, sums of money, and keys, which complete and signify the completion of the buying and selling process. It is after completion normally that the buyer takes possession of the house.

Compulsory purchase   If an official body—like a council—wants a house it can get it, under Act of Parliament, even if the owner does not want to yield it. This is compulsory purchase (it might better be called 'compulsory sale').

Conveyancing   The legal term for the transferring of the ownership of a house, or land.

Covenant   An undertaking or promise binding on the owner of a dwelling set out formally in a legal document.

Deed of conveyance   The legal document which transfers the ownership of a house, or land, from seller to buyer.

Development plan   Comprehensive proposals by a local authority for the future of areas under its control. The housebuyer's concern must be to see that such proposals do not affect the house he is thinking of buying, or not injuriously.

Draft contract   The document which the seller, or his solicitor, sends to the buyer's solicitor setting out the conditions of sale relating to the proposed transaction between the two. The sending of this document, and the buyer's receiving it, mark the beginning of the serious examination of all the circumstances which will confirm the buyer—or not—in a decision to proceed with the deal.

Easements   Ownership of a house may confer a right of way through a neighbouring property or there may be a right of light which prevents a neighbour putting up anything which would unreasonably cut out natural light. Such rights are called *easements* by lawyers.

Interest rates   Interest is the charge made by a building society for lending the money for purchase of a house. The higher the interest rate the higher will be the borrower's monthly mortgage repayments. The recommended mortgage interest rate at the time of publication of this book is $8\frac{1}{2}$ per cent. You will be lucky to get a mortgage at a rate lower than this, and you may have to accept a higher rate if the building society isn't very enthusiastic about the house, if the purchase has unusual features or if the mortgage arrangement is out of the ordinary. A mortgage may be arranged at a fixed, i.e. non-variable rate of interest, but such an arrangement is not common. It is important to understand the effect of levels of interest rate on monthly repayments. If you borrow £4000 over 19 years at $8\frac{1}{2}$ per cent your monthly repayments will be £36. If you borrow the same sum over the same period at $9\frac{1}{2}$ per cent you will pay £2.50 a month more—a rise in outgoings of about 7 per cent.

Land Registry   See *Registered* below.

Letter of acceptance   Sometimes known as offer of advance. It is the communication from the building society stating the mortgage the society is prepared to give you.

National House-Builders Registration Council   This body provides, in effect, a guarantee scheme covering buyers of new houses built by builders registered with the council against defects and trouble after they have moved in. The scheme also covers the contingency of a builder going bankrupt before he has finished a house for a client or for some other reason failing to complete the job.

Outline planning permission   The preliminary to planning permission.

Planning permission   Permission from a local planning authority allowing 'development' to be carried out. 'Development' is defined as 'the carrying out of building, engineering, mining, or other operations, in, on, over or under land, or the making of any material change in the use of any building or other land'. If you are having a house built you must have planning permission. If you intend to divide an existing house into two you will need planning permission. If you intend to add an annexe, make a new drive, build a garage, a high fence, add a bay window or a porch or alter the external appearance of the house you may need planning permission. One of the things you must make sure of in buying a house is that any such work carried out in the past was done with planning permission. Whether or not planning permission is necessary for any particular work, other rules *must* be observed—bye-laws and building regulations—information on which, as with planning permssion, you can get from the local council offices.

Redemption charges   A financial penalty imposed by a building society when a borrower clears his mortgage early. The penalty is often three months' interest, but practice varies. Some societies do not enforce redemption charges: others impose them only if the mortgage is repaid in the first five years: others have a similar three-year rule: others waive the charge if the borrower takes out his next mortgage with the same society. Redemption charges are not easily to be justified, and there is a sentiment that they ought to be abolished. The first-time buyer is not likely to care very much about what may happen in six or seven years' time when he will want to sell the house, redeem the mortgage and buy another place. But if he happens to consult this book again at that juncture, the advice it offers is to protest against the charge and demand a waiver: the rules of the society probably provide for waiving and if the borrower is firm enough about it he may prevail.

Registered   When a house is described as 'registered' it and its ownership and other details about it are recorded in a file at the Land Registry and can easily be checked by a solicitor. If it is 'unregistered' it is not so recorded, and naturally a solicitor's inquiries are made more difficult. That is why higher fees are charged by solicitors for dealing with an unregistered house. The saving in fees resulting from a house being registered is somewhat offset by the fact that fees have to be paid to the Land Registry when the house is sold to a new owner. Also if a house is being registered for the first time a registration fee has to be paid.

Rates   The charge made on a householder to help meet the cost of local council services. Generally speaking, the more valuable the house in a district the more the owner will pay in rates. Rates are payable every half year as a rule, the householder going to the council offices to pay, sending a cheque or arranging payment through a standing order with his bank. Some councils accept monthly payments, which makes budgetting easier. Rates vary slightly year by year as councils' annual budgets change. In buying a house a question that must be asked is 'How much are the present rates?' The figure will probably be between £3 and £6 a month and a building society will take the liability into account in deciding how big a mortgage the buyer can afford to repay. In other words, the buyer's future obligations as a ratepayer will reduce his mortgage capability by the margin represented by outgoings of, say, £3 to £6 a month. In addition to council rates ('general rates'), a householder must also pay a water rate. The bill for this comes separately, and is very small—four or five pounds a year.

Road charges The house you buy will stand in a street. You will expect the street to be made up and kept in good repair. This costs money, and as a houseowner with a frontage to the street you may receive a bill from the local council to meet part of the cost. Such a demand is known as 'road charges'. Nearly always some arrangement in the past has ensured that no such charge will be made on you and the other houseowners in the street, and that the council will maintain the road out of its own funds. However, this may not be so in some cases and one of the things to be found out before committing yourself to buy a house is whether or not you may be liable to road charges in the future.

Stamp duty A Government charge on transaction in property. Stamp duty on the transfer of ownership of houses is charged on dwellings costing £5500 or more: between £5500 and £7000 the rate of the levy is $\frac{1}{2}$ per cent of price; above £7000 the rate is 1 per cent of price.

Title Ownership. 'Investigating title' means checking that the seller of a house is indeed the full and proper owner of it.

Title deeds Documents establishing the ownership of property.

Unregistered See *Registered*.

INDEX